HERBS LOVE TOMATOES, PEPPERS, ONIONS & ZUCCHINI

HERBS LOVE TOMATOES, PEPPERS, ONIONS & ZUCCHINI

A
Fresh from the Garden
Cookbook

RUTH BASS

ILLUSTRATED BY MARY RICH

STOREY
BOOKS

Schoolhouse Road
Pownal, Vermont 05261

The mission of Storey Communications is to serve our customers
by publishing practical information that encourages personal independence
in harmony with the environment.

Edited by Pamela Lappies and Jeanée Ledoux
Cover and text design by Meredith Maker
Cover and interior illustrations by Mary Rich
Text production by Susan Bernier
Indexed by Nan Badgett, Word•a•bil•i•ty

Storey books are available for special premium and promotional uses and for customized editions. For further information, please call Storey's Custom Publishing Department at 800-793-9396.

Printed in The United States by R. R. Donnelley
10 9 8 7 6 5 4 3 2 1

**Library of Congress
Cataloging-in-Publication Data**

Bass, Ruth, 1934-
 Herbs love tomatoes, peppers, onions & zucchini: a fresh from the garden cookbook / by Ruth Bass.
  p. cm.
 Includes index.
 ISBN 1-58017-290-3
 1. Cookery (Herbs) 2. Cookery (Vegetables)
I. Title.
TX819.H4 B38823 2000
 641.6'57-dc21   00-028514

Contents

Introduction

Herbs infuse basic ingredients with new aromas, taste sensations, colors, and freshness. Garlic, thyme, basil, and parsley are old friends to most cooks. Sage, savory, marjoram, chervil, lemon verbena, rose petals, oregano, cardamom, cilantro, dill, rosemary, and other herbs also cry out to make your favorite foods even better, to give old recipes new twists.

The versatility of herbs is welcome come midsummer since everyone has a garden overflowing with tomatoes, peppers, onions, and especially zucchini and other squash. Whether you grow your own produce or buy it year-round, herbs can help you to bring interesting dishes to the table every time.

The tomato world is enormous, and the connoisseur learns that different varieties neither look nor taste alike. Pasta sauce is improved by at least a few Italian plum-style tomatoes. For salads, yellow pear shapes mix nicely with red or pink cherry-style tomatoes. These fruits also come egg shaped, fluted, and striped. Whatever their shapes or colors, their connection with herbs is like that of love and marriage — they just go together.

Tomatoes can be finicky in the garden, but anyone who has savored a homegrown tomato is willing to pamper these plants. Tomatoes like plenty of light, fertile soil, and organic matter. As the vines climb skyward, train them with cages or stakes.

The world of peppers rivals tomatoland for variety. There are big, glossy, colorful, sweet peppers that can be eaten like apples; medium hot, stubby peppers that look deceptively innocent; and blazing hot, bonnet-shaped peppers that should be used with the ultimate care. Sweet peppers can be domineering, and hot peppers shove all other flavors out of the way if they aren't used with discretion. The trick is to take advantage of each pepper's good traits and meld it with herbs that soften its personality.

Peppers are low-maintenance plants. The danger comes in giving them too much care. Overfertilized peppers develop a wonderfully bushy shape and dozens of shiny leaves, but they may fail to bloom, leaving you with empty branches.

Members of the Allium family — onions, shallots, chives, scallions, leeks, and garlic — are at home with most herbs in and out of the garden. And, indeed, since they're not much trouble and don't take up much space, they ought to have a prominent place in your kitchen garden.

Spanish, yellow, and red onions can be grown from seeds, plants, or sets. Perennial chives, with their round lavender flowers appearing early in the season, work nicely in a flower or rock garden. Garlic varies from one garden to the next; some gardeners plant it in the fall for the next year's harvest. Shallots are prolific: Just poke a few from the kitchen supply into the ground, 12 inches apart.

What gardener needs advice about growing zucchini? Ever-producing vines drive some gardeners to leave baskets of unwanted bounty on neighbors' doorsteps. Rest assured that the addition of herbs can make each zucchini dish delicious and different from the last.

For the more mellow winter squashes, generally much brighter in color than they are in flavor, herbs provide pizazz. Perk up butternut squash with dill and sage. Add mint and a little citrus to acorn squash to wake up your tastebuds.

Tomato Omelette with Marjoram

You can cut cherry tomatoes in half, heat a little olive oil in a small skillet, put tomatoes in cut side down, then serve them sprinkled with fresh marjoram next to eggs. Or you can turn out this omelette, which combines tomatoes, marjoram, and farmer cheese, which is slightly tart and crumbly.

2 tablespoons extra virgin olive oil	8 eggs
3 fresh ripe tomatoes, chopped	¼ cup water
3 large shallots, minced	Salt and freshly ground
1 cup farmer cheese, crumbled	black pepper
2 teaspoons minced fresh marjoram	4 tablespoons butter

1. Heat the oil in a skillet. Add the tomatoes and shallots and cook until soft, stirring frequently. Remove the pan from the heat and stir in the cheese and marjoram. Set aside.
2. Beat the eggs with a fork until they are light and well blended. Add the water plus salt and pepper to taste.
3. Melt the butter in a clean skillet; when it is hot and foamy, pour in the egg mixture. Cook until set, lifting the edge occasionally to let the liquid run under the cooked portion.
4. Spoon the tomato mixture across the middle of the omelet. Fold the sides toward the middle and let cook another minute or so.

4 SERVINGS

Tomato Pesto Frittata

Omelettes are fun, versatile, and tasty. Frittatas are elegant. You pull that puffed-up, golden dish out of the oven, and oohs and aahs are yours. For a special breakfast or a quick but out-of-the-ordinary supper, put this frittata with pesto together in a few minutes.

4 tablespoons extra virgin olive oil
2 onions, sliced
Salt
3 ripe tomatoes, peeled, seeded, and chopped
1 garlic clove, minced
5 eggs
Freshly ground black pepper
2 tablespoons chopped fresh basil
¼ cup chopped fresh parsley
2 tablespoons grated Parmesan cheese
1 teaspoon finely chopped pine nuts
2 tablespoons butter

1. In a large skillet, heat the oil and add the onions and a little salt. Cover the pan and simmer over low heat for 5 minutes. Uncover and cook until soft and golden.

2. Add the tomatoes and minced garlic, stirring to coat all ingredients. Let simmer for 15 minutes, then drain off the oil. Set the vegetables aside.
3. Preheat the oven to 350°F. In a large bowl, beat the eggs and add the tomato and onion mixture, pepper to taste, basil, parsley, cheese, and pine nuts. Combine well.
4. Place the butter in a 10-inch layer cake pan and put it in the oven until the butter melts. Swirl the butter to cover the sides of the pan. Pour in the frittata mixture. Bake for about 15 minutes or until the eggs are no longer runny.
5. Loosen the edges and slide the frittata onto a serving plate, or serve from the pan, cutting pie-shaped pieces.

4 SERVINGS

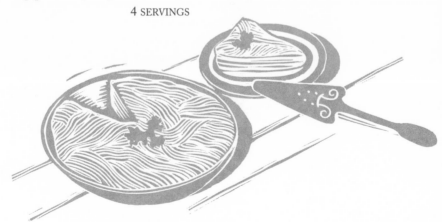

Sweet Million Appetizer

Sweet Million tomatoes were the next step after the Sweet 100s, gems in the world of what we generically refer to as cherry tomatoes. They grow in clusters like grapes, produce prolifically, and do not crack in late season the way some of their cousins do. They are pretty and tasty as a quick hors d'oeuvre or salad, especially when accompanied by fragrant basil.

1 quart Sweet Millions or other cherry tomato
5 large basil leaves
¼ pound fresh mozzarella
Freshly ground black pepper
1 sprig parsley
Extra virgin olive oil

1. Wash the tomatoes, pat them dry, and slice off the stem ends.
2. Arrange the tomatoes on an attractive plate and put a snip of basil on each one.
3. Slice the mozzarella ¼-inch thick and cut into squares smaller than the tomatoes. Place a square on each tomato.
4. Top with a bit of pepper to taste and a bit of the parsley sprig. Add another small square of mozzarella and another bit of pepper and parsley. Drizzle the oil over the whole plate and let stand for at least a half hour before serving at room temperature.

4 SERVINGS AS A SALAD, 8 AS AN HORS D'OEUVRE

Also called St. Josephwort, basil is held in high esteem in the East but is regarded as an agent of evil in Crete.

Tomato Thyme Cocktail

This is one of those recipes that seems simple but delivers the goods. Ordinary tomato juice doesn't quite cut it after you've tried this version with thyme, which comes from Grandma's cookbook. You can cook up as many tomatoes as you want if you're willing to can the juice.

3–4 pounds ripe tomatoes
2 teaspoons chopped fresh thyme, or 1 teaspoon dried
Juice of 1½ lemons
1 teaspoon salt
½ cup sugar
Pinch of ground cloves

1. Cut up the tomatoes. In a large enameled or stainless-steel kettle, combine the tomatoes and the thyme. Heat them to boiling and cook gently until soft.
2. Put the cooked tomatoes through a food mill to remove the bulky part of the pulp. Next, put the mixture through a large strainer to remove all seeds and pulp.
3. Add the lemon juice, salt, sugar, and cloves. Chill before serving.

1 QUART

Tomato, Basil, and Barley Soup

The sweetness of tomatoes with the heartiness of barley makes a filling soup for a winter day. This one adds the flavor of basil and will take care of a small crowd, so put it in a ceramic pot and keep it hot on a warming tray.

4 *tablespoons softened butter*
2 *medium sweet onions, chopped*
2 *quarts water*
8 *medium tomatoes, peeled and chopped (4 cups)*
1 *cup barley*
1 *large garlic clove on a toothpick*
2 *tablespoons chopped fresh basil*
Salt and freshly ground pepper

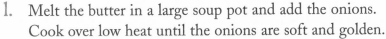

1. Melt the butter in a large soup pot and add the onions. Cook over low heat until the onions are soft and golden.
2. Fill another pot with the water and bring to a boil. Drop the tomatoes in and remove after a few seconds, reserving the boiling water. Rinse the tomatoes with cold water and peel. Add to the onions the tomatoes, boiling water, barley, garlic, and basil.
3. Simmer, covered, for 1–1½ hours. Remove the garlic, add salt and pepper to taste, and serve.

3 QUARTS

Parsleyed Tomato Bisque

Tomato soup is ubiquitous. From the Campbell's every American kid has enjoyed with a grilled cheese sandwich to versions found in far-off lands, it warms us. This version marries tomatoes with bay leaves and parsley.

8   tomatoes, chopped (2½ cups)
1   teaspoon sugar
1   cup water
1   sweet white onion, chopped
3   tablespoons softened butter
2   garlic cloves, put through a press
1   bay leaf
½   cup chopped fresh parsley
3   slices crusty Italian bread
4   cups low-fat milk
Salt and freshly ground black pepper

1. In a large soup pot, cook the tomatoes and sugar in the water at medium heat for 20 minutes or until the tomatoes are soft.
2. In a separate pan, cook the onion in the butter until it is soft and golden, not browned. Add to the soup pot, along with the garlic, bay leaf, and parsley. Cook at medium heat for 5 minutes. Remove the bay leaf.

3. Using a blender or food processor, make fine bread crumbs from the crusty bread. You should have about 1 cup. Set aside. Then, in the same container, purée the soup mixture and return to the pot.
4. Combine the bread crumbs and milk in a separate saucepan, and heat to the scalding point (when the milk will just start to skin over). Add the milk and crumbs to the soup pot, stir well, and reheat to the boiling point.
5. Add salt and pepper to taste and serve in heated bowls.

6 SERVINGS

Andalusian Gazpacho

Those who cheered on the world's athletes at the 1992 Olympic Games discovered a special treat at the sidewalk cafés of Barcelona: a silky smooth gazpacho that was cold, refreshing, and almost the color of cream of tomato soup. Here's how they made it:

3 *garlic cloves*
3 *slices white bread*
2 *green peppers*
6–9 *tomatoes (about 3 pounds)*
6 *tablespoons white wine vinegar*
5 *tablespoons olive oil*
Salt and freshly ground black pepper
A dash of sugar
1 *cucumber*
1 *onion*
1 *red pepper*
¼ *cup chopped fresh chervil*

I. Mash the garlic cloves. Remove the crusts from the bread and cut into cubes. Chop one of the peppers and peel the tomatoes. Cut 2 slices from one of the tomatoes and reserve.

2. Put the garlic, bread, chopped pepper, tomatoes, vinegar, oil, salt and pepper to taste, and sugar in a food processor or blender and give it a whirl. If the mixture seems thick, add a little cold water to make it soupy. Chill.
3. Finely dice the cucumber, onion, red and green peppers, the chervil, and the 2 reserved slices of tomato. Put each into a separate serving bowl.
4. Put a couple of ice cubes in chilled soup cups and pour the soup over them. Garnish with the diced vegetables.

6 SERVINGS

Dilly Tomatoes

You think: tomatoes and basil. No, tomatoes and oregano. No, tomatoes and parsley. Ah, but then there's the combination of tomatoes with dill. It appears that the tomato, lushest of the garden vegetables, can cozy up to any one of the herbs — or several at once.

4 large ripe tomatoes
½ cup plain yogurt
2 tablespoons snipped fresh dillweed
¼ cup mayonnaise
1 scallion, minced (2 tablespoons)
Salt and freshly ground pepper
1 garlic clove, minced
2 tablespoons butter

1. Preheat the broiler. Core the tomatoes and remove a thin slice from the blossom end.
2. Combine the yogurt, dill, mayonnaise, scallion, and a little salt. Refrigerate the mixture.
3. Cut the tomatoes in half, crosswise. Place them cut side up on a broiling pan and season with the minced garlic and the salt and pepper to taste. Dot with the butter.

4. Broil 3 inches from the heat for 5 minutes or until the tomatoes are heated through.
5. To serve, top with the chilled yogurt mixture.

8 SERVINGS

Dill derives its name from the Norse word dilla, *which means "to lull."*

Tomato Bean Blend with Thyme

Black and red make a stunning salad combination, especially if the vegetables are arranged on a black dish and sprinkled with herbs. This should be prepared in a serving dish no more than 10 inches in diameter so that you'll have a number of layers and the flavors will blend.

2 large red bell peppers	*⅔ cup fine, unflavored bread crumbs*
8 medium tomatoes	*1½ tablespoons grated Romano cheese*
½ cup sun-dried tomatoes in olive oil	*4 tablespoons extra virgin olive oil*
3 tablespoons minced fresh parsley	*1½ teaspoons white wine vinegar*
2 tablespoons minced fresh thyme	*1 can (16 ounces) black beans*
2 tablespoons minced fresh oregano	*Salt and freshly ground black pepper*
	1 tablespoon capers

1. Preheat the broiler. Slice the red peppers lengthwise, removing stems and seeds. Place the peppers skin side up on a broiling pan and pop them under the broiler for 5 to 7 minutes, charring them.
2. Place the blackened peppers in a paper bag, close it tightly, and set aside for 10 minutes.
3. In the meantime, set the oven at 375°F. Remove the stem and blossom ends from the tomatoes and cut into ¼-inch slices. Drain the sun-dried tomatoes and finely chop. Combine the parsley, thyme, and oregano in a small bowl. Combine the bread crumbs and cheese in a separate bowl.

4. Open the bag of peppers, taking care not to get burned by escaping steam. When they are cool enough to handle, peel the peppers and slice into strips.
5. Mix the oil and vinegar, and pour half the mixture into a bake-and-serve dish. Add a layer of tomatoes and a thin layer of black beans. Sprinkle with some of the sun-dried tomatoes, herb mixture, and pepper to taste.
6. Add a layer of pepper strips. Cover them with more tomato slices, beans, sun-dried tomatoes, herbs, pepper, and salt to taste. Continue until all the vegetables have been used. Pour the rest of the oil and vinegar over the top; add the capers and the bread crumb mixture. Bake 30 minutes or until the top is browned and the tomatoes are soft.
7. Cool on the counter, then refrigerate. Serve chilled.

4 SERVINGS

Green Beans with Tomatoes and Savory

If the garden behaves nicely and produces slender, crisp green beans just as the tomatoes are becoming fat and red, this salad with parsley and savory will be very special. It can be served at room temperature or well chilled.

About a pound of green beans
4 medium tomatoes
1 small sweet onion, chopped
4 tablespoons extra virgin olive oil
Juice of half a large lemon
1 garlic clove, minced
½ cup chopped fresh parsley
2 tablespoons chopped fresh savory
3 tablespoons pine nuts
Salt and freshly ground pepper

1. Fill a pot with water and bring to a boil. Meanwhile, snip the ends off the beans, but leave them whole. When the water is boiling, drop the tomatoes in for a few seconds, remove, then rinse with cold water and peel. Chop and place in a strainer to let some of the juice run off.
2. Combine the onion, oil, lemon juice, garlic, parsley, savory, and pine nuts in a small jar with a tightly fitting lid. Shake well; then let stand.

3. Cook the beans about 5 minutes over medium heat in a saucepan with water to cover. They should be crisp. Drain, rinse with cold water to stop the cooking, and drain again.
4. Place the beans and tomatoes in a salad bowl. Pour the dressing mixture over the vegetables and toss gently. The flavors should be allowed to blend for at least 15 minutes before serving.
5. Serve at room temperature or chilled.

6 SALAD SERVINGS

Marinated Vegetables with Tarragon

When the produce looks picture-perfect in either the garden or the supermarket, vegetables need no cooking. Don't boil — marinate. Almost any vegetable you like can be substituted in this dish: Try slim slices of red onion, zucchini, or cauliflower, for instance.

¾ cup extra virgin olive oil
½ cup rosemary or tarragon vinegar
2 tablespoons lemon juice
4 tablespoons chopped scallions,
  green and white parts
2 teaspoons minced fresh tarragon
Salt and freshly ground pepper

2 teaspoons sugar
2 medium tomatoes, chopped (1 cup)
1 cup halved cherry tomatoes
1 cup pea pods, trimmed
1 cup coarsely chopped unpeeled
  zucchini

1. In a medium bowl, whisk together the oil, vinegar, lemon juice, scallions, tarragon, salt and pepper to taste, and sugar.
2. Arrange the tomatoes, pea pods, and zucchini in a shallow dish and add the marinade. Cover with plastic wrap and refrigerate for 3 to 24 hours. Stir at least once.
3. Drain off the marinade before serving.

4–6 SERVINGS

Rosemary or Tarragon Vinegar

This recipe, taken from *Herbal Vinegar* by Maggie Oster, can be adapted for use with any herb.

> 1 *cup loosely packed fresh rosemary or tarragon leaves*
> 2 *cups sherry vinegar or white wine vinegar*

1. Place the herbs in a clean, sterilized jar and use a spoon to bruise them slightly. Pour the vinegar over the herbs and cover the jar tightly.
2. Put the jar in a dark place at room temperature to let the herb-vinegar mixture steep. Shake the jar every few days and taste the vinegar after a week. If the flavor is not strong enough, let it stand for another 1 to 3 weeks, checking the flavor weekly. If an even stronger flavor is desired, repeat the steeping process with fresh herbs.
3. When the flavor is right, strain the vinegar, fill a clean, sterilized bottle, cap tightly, and label.

2 CUPS

19

Herbed Tomatoes with Avocados

These tomatoes blend with herbs to make an ideal buffet dish that can be made a day ahead of time. Well in advance, buy the dark-skinned avocados for this dish. Few things are less flavorful than an unripe avocado.

10 *avocados, peeled and cut into chunks*
Juice of half a lemon
1 *large jar (64 ounces) of artichoke hearts, including liquid*
4 *large tomatoes, chopped coarsely*
5 *stalks of celery, chopped, including leaves*
2 *cups chopped onion*
½ *cup sun-dried tomatoes*
3 *tablespoons chopped chives*
2 *garlic cloves, minced*
2 *tablespoons chopped fresh tarragon*
1 *teaspoon chopped fresh thyme*

1. Place the avocado chunks in a large bowl and toss with the lemon juice.
2. Add the artichokes and liquid, tomatoes, celery, onion, sun-dried tomatoes, chives, garlic, tarragon, and thyme. Toss gently, cover with plastic wrap, and refrigerate for up to 24 hours.
3. Drain liquid before serving.

ABOUT 6 QUARTS OF VEGETABLES

Tarragon Tomato Salad Dressing

If you make your own French-style dressing, it will taste fresh and perhaps carry fewer calories to the salad. You can substitute basil, oregano, thyme, or chervil for the tarragon.

¾ cup tomato juice
¼ cup white wine vinegar
½ cup yogurt
 1 tablespoon Worcestershire sauce
 1 scallion, chopped
 1 tablespoon minced fresh tarragon
¼ teaspoon prepared mustard
    Freshly ground pepper

1. Combine the juice, vinegar, yogurt, Worcestershire, scallion, tarragon, mustard, and pepper to taste in a blender and process until smooth. Refrigerate for an hour so that the flavors will blend.
2. To store, refrigerate in a tightly covered container.

1¾ CUPS

Stuffed Tomatoes Niçoise

If it says *Niçoise* (knee-SWAHZ), it's bound to have black olives, garlic, olive oil, and anchovies. This recipe has all those things and more.

6 *large tomatoes*
2 *tablespoons olive oil*
6 *shallots, chopped*
1 *tablespoon anchovy paste or mashed anchovies*
2 *tablespoons chopped black olives*
1 *tablespoon chopped fresh basil*
1 *garlic clove, minced*
2 *tablespoons chopped fresh parsley*
1 *teaspoon capers, chopped*
Salt and freshly ground pepper
1 *can (7 ounces) white-meat tuna*
¼ *cup dry white wine*
1 *cup cooked pastini or orzo*
    (½ cup uncooked)
¼ *cup fine bread crumbs*
1 *tablespoon butter*

1. Preheat the oven to 400°F. Slice the tops off the tomatoes and hollow them out, reserving the pulp. Chop the pulp.
2. Heat the oil in a pan, add the shallots, and cook until they are golden. Stir in the tomato pulp, anchovy paste, olives, basil, garlic, parsley, capers, and salt and pepper to taste. Flake the tuna and add to the mixture. Blend in the wine.
3. Cook for 2 minutes, then add the cooked pasta. Fill the tomatoes with the mixture. Top with bread crumbs and dot with butter.
4. Bake about 15 minutes or until the tomatoes are cooked through.

6 SERVINGS

Ancient Romans and Greeks believed
that wearing garlands of parsley
would prevent drunkenness.

Not-So-Welsh Rarebit

Commonly called "rabbit," the rarebit is usually a somewhat sharp, cheesy concoction served on toast for lunch or a simple supper. This one includes parsley, tomatoes, and a Texas-style whammy.

> 4 large ripe tomatoes
> 2 medium onions
> 1 medium green pepper, seeded
> ¾ teaspoon cayenne
> A few drops of hot chili oil
> 2 tablespoons butter
> 1 cup cubed sharp cheddar cheese
> 1 tablespoon minced fresh parsley and sprigs for garnish
> 1 teaspoon mustard
> 1 teaspoon Worcestershire sauce
> ½ cup milk
> Sourdough or Italian bread

1. Fill a pot with water and bring to a boil. Drop the tomatoes in for less than a minute, remove, rinse with cold water, peel, and chop. Chop the onions and pepper.
2. In a saucepan, combine the tomatoes, onions, pepper, cayenne, and hot chili oil. Cook over medium heat for about 30 minutes. If the tomatoes are very

juicy, drain off most of the liquid. Let the mixture cool before making the cheese sauce.

3. In a double boiler, melt the butter, add the cheese, and stir until the cheese has melted. Add the parsley, mustard, Worcestershire sauce, and milk.

4. Cook, stirring frequently, until thickened. Add the tomato sauce and reheat. Serve hot on toasted sourdough or crisp Italian bread. Garnish with parsley sprigs.

4 TO 6 SERVINGS

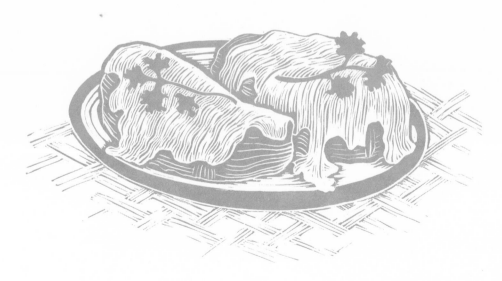

Tomato Basil Bake

Vegetarians can make a meal out of this. It's also a perfect accompaniment to a simple chicken or veal dish, providing vegetables and potatoes in one casserole, blended with basil.

5 tablespoons extra virgin olive oil
3 ripe but firm tomatoes
6 medium potatoes
3 sweet onions, sliced paper-thin (2 cups)
¼ cup minced fresh basil
2 garlic cloves, minced
Salt and freshly ground pepper
½ cup grated Parmesan cheese
¼ cup grated Romano cheese
½ cup water

1. Preheat the oven to 400°F and lightly grease a 13 x 9-inch baking dish with 1 tablespoon of the oil.
2. Fill a pot with water and bring to a boil. Drop the tomatoes in for less than a minute, remove, rinse with cold water, and peel. Dice them, removing most of the seeds. Peel the potatoes and slice them ¼-inch thick.

3. In a bowl, combine the remaining oil, onion, tomato, basil, garlic, salt and pepper to taste, and grated cheeses. Mix in the water. Add the potatoes and toss to mix well.
4. Put the mixture in the baking dish and bake on an upper shelf of the oven for an hour, or until the potatoes are done. The mixture should be stirred after 20 minutes and again after another 20 minutes.

6 SERVINGS

Basil derives its name from the Greek word basileus, *which means "king."*

Creamy Tomato Sauce with Herbs

If you have leftover chicken or turkey, or you'd like to give your tuna casserole a change of direction, substitute this herbed sauce for a plain white sauce. You can also use it over vegetables, such as fresh asparagus on toast.

> 2 tablespoons butter
> 2 tablespoons flour
> 1 cup milk, at room temperature
> ½ teaspoon salt
> Freshly ground pepper
> 2 large ripe tomatoes, chopped (about 2 cups)
> 1 sweet onion, minced
> 1 tablespoon minced fresh basil
> 1 teaspoon minced fresh parsley
> ¼ teaspoon minced fresh thyme
> 2 garlic cloves, minced

1. In the microwave, melt the butter in a quart-size glass measuring cup or other container tall enough to keep the butter from splattering.
2. Stir in the flour and microwave for 2 minutes, stirring after the first minute.
3. Add the milk slowly, stirring continuously. Microwave for 4 minutes, stirring after each minute. Stir in the salt and add pepper to taste. Set aside.

4. Over low heat, cook the tomatoes and onion for about 10 minutes. Add the basil, parsley, thyme, and garlic and simmer another 2 minutes.
5. Purée the tomato mixture in a blender or food processor and combine with the white sauce.

ABOUT 3 CUPS

Red Sauce with Basil for Pasta

Tomato sauce comes in a thousand guises. With most of the recipes, you can add or subtract ingredients to get the perfect blend. This one provides a start, and the result can be used on spaghetti or in lasagna. Sautéed ground beef can be added to make a meat sauce, and other herbs can be added. The sauce also freezes beautifully for winter use. If it's a little watery — sometimes a tomato can be too juicy — add a can of tomato paste.

¼ cup butter
¼ cup extra virgin olive oil
2 onions, coarsely chopped
4 garlic cloves, chopped
¼ cup chopped fresh parsley
4 pounds ripe tomatoes
1 stalk celery with leaves
¼ cup basil leaves, packed
Salt and freshly ground pepper

1. In a large saucepan, melt the butter, add the oil, and sauté the onions until they are golden but not browned. Stir in the garlic and parsley and cook over low heat for 3 minutes.
2. Put the tomatoes, celery, and basil in a food processor or blender and purée. Add salt and pepper to taste. Pour into the saucepan and cook slowly for at least 2 hours.
3. If you like a chunky sauce, serve it as is. If you prefer smooth, put it through a blender or a food mill.

2 QUARTS

*High in chlorophyll, parsley leaves
are natural breath fresheners.*

Pesto Tomato Pasta

The green sauce — with basil as the major ingredient — has become a staple for American cooks. Here it combines with summer's best tomatoes and rotelle for a tasty treat.

¾ *cup extra virgin olive oil*
½ *cup balsamic vinegar*
2 *cups fresh basil leaves*
½ *cup fresh parsley*
4 *large garlic cloves*
Salt and freshly ground pepper
8 *large tomatoes, peeled and cut into quarters*
1 *pound rotelle or other pasta*
½ *cup grated Parmesan cheese*

1. Put a large pot of water on the stove to boil.
2. Place the oil and vinegar in a food processor and add the basil, parsley, garlic, and salt and pepper to taste. Purée.
3. Add the tomatoes and process until they are coarsely chopped. Refrigerate the mixture.

4. Cook the pasta in boiling water according to the directions on the package. Drain.
5. While the pasta is hot, add the tomato mixture and toss gently. Serve immediately with Parmesan cheese while the pasta is still warm.

6 TO 8 SERVINGS

Herbed Spaghetti Sauce in the Raw

An elegant way to prepare spaghetti sauce when tomatoes are red and lush and sweet at midsummer is not to cook the sauce at all. Just add fresh herbs and serve.

> 2 pounds fresh, really ripe tomatoes
> 1 pound linguini or other spaghetti
> ½ cup fresh basil leaves, packed
> 2 garlic cloves, minced
> 3 tablespoons finely chopped fresh parsley
> ¼ cup extra virgin olive oil
> Juice of 1 lemon
> Salt and freshly ground pepper
> ¼ cup grated Parmesan
> ¼ cup grated Romano

1. The tomatoes should be at room temperature, neither hot from the garden nor chilled. Chop them, then place in a strainer. Let drain for at least 15 minutes.
2. In a large pot, drop the linguini into boiling water and make sure the strands are separated. Cook according to taste or the directions on the package.

3. Cut the basil leaves into short strips. Place the tomatoes in a bowl, add the garlic, basil, parsley, oil, and lemon juice, and toss gently. Add salt and pepper to taste.

4. Drain the linguini, place it in a warmed pasta bowl, pour the sauce over the top, and mix lightly. Serve with the grated cheeses.

4 SERVINGS

Spicy Green Tomato Bread

Those who live where frost pounces suddenly in the fall often mourn the loss of all those glossy, green tomatoes that won't get time to ripen. Or, they can harvest a bushel or two and cook them up with oregano and spices.

2¼ cups unbleached white flour
1½ teaspoons baking powder
1 teaspoon baking soda
¼ teaspoon salt
¼ teaspoon ground nutmeg
1 teaspoon ground ginger
1 tablespoon minced fresh oregano
2 eggs
⅓ cup honey
⅓ cup melted, unsalted butter
⅔ cup apple cider (preferably without preservatives)
2–3 green tomatoes, diced (1–1¼ cups)

1. Preheat the oven to 325°F and butter a large loaf pan. Sift the flour, baking powder, soda, salt, nutmeg, ginger, and oregano together.
2. In a large bowl, beat the eggs, add the honey, and beat again. Add the butter and cider and keep beating. Stir in the tomatoes.

3. Fold in the dry ingredients until everything is combined. Pour the batter into the greased pan and bake about an hour or until the top springs back when touched and the edges are pulling away from the sides of the pan.

4. Cool on a rack for 10 minutes in the pan, then remove from pan to cool completely on the rack.

1 LOAF

Cilantro Tomato Sandwich

BLTs are melt-in-your-mouth sandwiches when they're made with garden tomatoes. Summer is the one time of the year that my family splurges on bacon. This cheesy, spiky version with cilantro and without lettuce is delicious, too.

3 tablespoons mayonnaise
1 teaspoon chili powder
4 ounces shredded cheddar cheese
4 slices rye bread
4 slices crisply cooked bacon
2 medium tomatoes, sliced
2 tablespoons minced fresh cilantro
Olive oil

1. Combine the mayonnaise, chili powder, and cheese and spread on 2 slices of the bread.
2. Add the bacon and the tomato slices and sprinkle with the cilantro. Add the second slice to each sandwich.
3. Wipe the surface of a large skillet with a little olive oil and heat the skillet. Add the sandwiches, cooking 3 to 4 minutes a side and taking great care not to lose the contents when turning.

2 SANDWICHES

Herbed Tomato Preserves

Here's a recipe that uses the smaller tomatoes in your garden.

1 teaspoon snipped fresh dill
1 bay leaf, crushed or snipped finely
1 teaspoon coriander seed
½ teaspoon allspice
½ teaspoon mustard seed
1-inch piece of ginger root, peeled

4 cups sugar
2 lemons, sliced thinly
¾ cup water
1½ quarts small red tomatoes,
    peeled (8 pounds)

1. Tie the herbs, spices, and ginger root in cheesecloth. Put in a large pot with the sugar, lemon slices, and water and simmer for 15 minutes.
2. Add the tomatoes and cook gently until almost transparent, stirring occasionally. Cover and let stand in a cool place for 12 to 18 hours.
3. Scrub 6 half-pint canning jars with two-piece lids. Boil the lids gently for 5 minutes and leave in the hot water.
4. Heat the tomato mixture to a boil. With a slotted spoon, scoop the mixture into the hot canning jars, leaving ½ inch of space at the top.
5. Remove the herb-and-spice bag. Boil the remaining syrup for 2 to 3 minutes, longer if it seems really watery. Pour the boiling hot syrup over the tomatoes, but not above the ½-inch point. Put on the lids and rings and process in a boiling water bath for 20 minutes.

6 HALF PINTS

Green Tomato Dill Pickle

In a year when frost comes long before the tomatoes have all ripened, it's time to make this pickle, which is both sweet and sharp and makes a beautiful addition to a Christmas basket of homemade goodies. While it's meant as a condiment, it can also be enjoyed as a sandwich filling.

¼ cup coarse salt
5 pounds green tomatoes, thinly sliced
½ pound onions, thinly sliced
4 teaspoons snipped fresh dillweed
½ teaspoon whole allspice
½ teaspoon whole cloves
½ teaspoon celery seed
1 large red pepper, chopped
1½ cups cider vinegar
¼ lemon, thinly sliced
½ tablespoon dry mustard
1½ cups granulated sugar
4 flower heads of dill

1. In a large kettle, add the salt to the tomatoes and onions and mix thoroughly. Let stand in a cool place for 10 hours minimum or overnight. Drain.

2. Place the dill and the spices in a cheesecloth bag. Combine the pepper, vinegar, lemon slices, mustard, and sugar with the tomatoes and onions and heat to a boil. Add the herb-and-spice bag and boil slowly for a half hour, stirring frequently.
3. Place one dill flower head in each of 4 clean, dry canning jars.
4. Remove the herb-and-spice bag and pour the tomato mixture into the jars. Seal and process in a pressure canner according to canner directions.
5. Remove jars, check seal a few hours later, and store.

4 PINTS

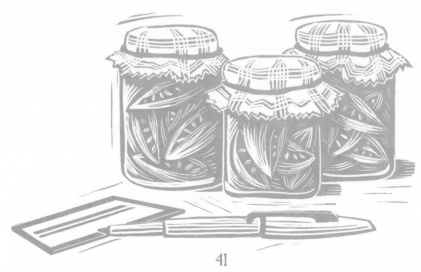

Fried Green Tomatoes

You probably saw the movie. Perhaps it led you to the book. The innovative restaurateurs of fiction had their Fried Green Tomatoes Restaurant and a recipe of the same name. This recipe is different (minus the bacon drippings and with the addition of cilantro and oregano), but still delicious — it works for breakfast, lunch, or dinner.

4 medium green tomatoes
3 tablespoons flour
1 teaspoon minced fresh cilantro
1 tablespoon minced fresh oregano
1 egg
6 tablespoons bread crumbs
3 tablespoons extra virgin
   olive oil

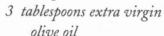

1. Slice the unpeeled tomatoes and place in a single layer on several thicknesses of paper towels. Let stand while preparing the herbs and dips.
2. In a shallow bowl or pie pan, combine the flour with the cilantro and oregano. In a separate bowl, beat the egg. Have the bread crumbs ready in another pie pan.
3. Heat the oil in a large skillet. Dip the tomato slices in the flour mixture, then into the egg, and then into the bread crumbs. Sauté in the skillet until browned; turn and cook until tender. Add olive oil as necessary.

6 SERVINGS

Stuffed Tomatoes Oregano

You can put nearly anything into a tomato once you've hollowed it out: tuna, chopped mushrooms with parsley and garlic, crab meat with mayonnaise, chopped avocado with lemon juice. Here's one tasty idea with a seafood theme.

> 1 pound small cooked shrimp, deveined and rinsed
> 1 teaspoon minced fresh oregano
> 2 teaspoons minced fresh parsley
> 8 Greek-style olives, pitted and chopped
> ½ cup extra virgin olive oil
> 1½ tablespoons finely chopped scallions, green
>   and white parts
> Juice of 1 lemon
> Salt and freshly ground black pepper
> 4 large ripe, firm tomatoes
> 4 curly lettuce leaves

1. Cut the shrimp into small pieces and combine with the oregano, parsley, olives, oil, scallions, lemon juice, and salt and pepper to taste. Mix well and set aside to let the flavors blend.
2. Cut a slice from the top of each tomato and a slim slice from the blossom end. Scoop out the pulp and place the tomato on a leaf of lettuce. Fill with the shrimp mixture and chill well before serving.

4 SERVINGS

Oregano gets its name from the Greek word origanum,
which means "joy of the mountains."

Tarragon Chicken and Tomatoes

Marinating chicken lets the flavors of fresh herbs and freshly picked produce absorb right into the meat and ensures tenderness. This marinade doubles as a sauce.

> *3 large boneless chicken breasts, cut in half*
> *8 tomatoes, peeled and chopped (4 cups)*
> *1 leek, chopped*
> *4 garlic cloves, minced*
> *2 scallions cut into 1-inch pieces, green and white parts*
> *1 tablespoon minced fresh parsley*
> *3 teaspoons minced fresh tarragon*
> *2 tablespoons light soy sauce*
> *1 cup chicken broth*
> *1 cup white wine*
> *Salt and freshly ground black pepper*

1. Carefully wash the chicken and remove all fat and membranes. Drain on paper towels and place in a single layer in a baking dish.
2. In a large bowl, combine the tomatoes, leek, garlic, scallions, parsley, tarragon, soy sauce, broth, wine, and salt and pepper to taste. Pour over the chicken. Cover tightly and refrigerate for at least 2 hours or as long as overnight, turning the chicken a few times.

3. Preheat the oven to 350°F. Pour off the marinade into a skillet and cook it down to about half its original volume. Pour the reduced sauce over the chicken and bake for 30 minutes, uncovering for the last 15 minutes.

6 SERVINGS

Veal with Tomatoes and Oregano

When veal scallopini is pale in color and pounded very thin, it cooks quickly and marvelously. Tomatoes, delicate but flavorful in the vegetable world, are an excellent companion for veal. (If you can't find plum tomatoes, try another kind.)

>   1 tablespoon butter
> 1½ tablespoons extra virgin olive oil
>   3 garlic cloves
> 3–4 tablespoons flour
>   Salt and freshly ground black pepper
>   1 pound veal scallopini
>   ½ cup dry white wine
>   3 ripe plum tomatoes, enough to make ½ cup
>   1 tablespoon chopped fresh oregano
>   2 tablespoons minced fresh parsley
>   2 tablespoons chopped black olives

1. Melt the butter in a large skillet and add the oil. When it is hot, sauté the garlic cloves whole until they are browned. Remove the garlic and discard.
2. Place the flour and ¼ teaspoon salt in a pie plate. Stir in pepper to taste and dredge the scallopini in the flour, shaking each piece to get rid of the excess.

With the heat turned to medium high, sauté the scallopini in the oil and butter, less than a minute a side. When the veal slices are cooked, transfer them to a warm plate and do another batch until all are finished.

3. Add the wine in the same skillet, and as it starts to bubble, scrape loose the bits of meat stuck to the pan. Add the chopped tomatoes, continuing to stir. Simmer about 15 minutes.

4. Return the scallopini to the pan along with the oregano and parsley and keep turning the slices until they are reheated. Add the black olives and serve on a warm platter.

4 SERVINGS

49

Beef, Tomato, and Leek Stir-Fry

Take a look at any assortment of ethnic cookbooks: The tomato shows up everywhere. This recipe has some Chinese ingredients, including soy sauce, and calls for stir-frying, which means the contents of the pan must be quickly scooped and turned over and over so that nothing sticks and everything cooks.

    2 *leeks*
    2 *white onions*
1½ *pounds sirloin tip beef*
    6 *tomatoes*
    1 *tablespoon sugar*
  ½ *inch fresh ginger root, shredded*
      Salt
1½ *cups beef stock*
  ½ *cup sherry or Chinese rice wine*
    3 *tablespoons peanut oil*
1½ *tablespoons peppercorns*
    4 *garlic cloves, chopped*
    2 *teaspoons minced fresh savory*
    2 *tablespoons light soy sauce*
3–4 *drops hot chili oil*
    1 *tablespoon cornstarch*
  ½ *cup minced fresh chervil*
3–4 *cups cooked rice*

1. Fill a pot with water and heat on high. While you are waiting for it to boil, cut off the green section of the leeks and discard. Slice the leeks in half lengthwise and soak in a pan of cool water for 10 minutes to make sure they are grit free. Slice the onions thinly and cube the beef.
2. Drop the tomatoes into the boiling water for 30 seconds, remove, rinse with cold water, and peel. Cut into quarters and sprinkle with the sugar. Remove the leeks from the water and slice into 1-inch pieces.
3. In a large saucepan or wok, combine the beef, onions, ginger, salt to taste, stock, and sherry or rice wine. Bring to a boil, reduce the heat, and simmer gently for about an hour, turning the contents every 15 minutes.
4. When the liquid has been reduced to a quarter of its original volume, remove the pan from the heat and take out the beef with a slotted spoon.
5. In a large skillet, heat the peanut oil. When it is hot, add the beef and peppercorns and stir-fry over high heat for 2 minutes. Add the leeks, garlic, savory, soy sauce, and hot chili oil and stir-fry another 2 minutes.
6. Add the tomatoes, turning and stirring continuously for another minute over high heat.
7. Combine the cornstarch with 3 tablespoons of water and add to the sauce in the wok or saucepan. Bring that to a boil, pour it over the beef and tomato mixture, and bring it to the bubbling point again. Add the chervil, toss, and serve with fluffy rice.

6 SERVINGS

Harold's Four-Alarm Chili

Sometimes chili con carne is a thick stew with beef, tomatoes, and beans. Sometimes it's Tex-Mex dynamite in a bowl. Harold's is the latter, made with chopped beef — he always insisted that purists don't use beans and don't use ground beef — fresh tomatoes, herbs, and jalapeños. It's hot and delicious. Make it in September and freeze it for December.

1 *large onion, chopped*
2 *tablespoons olive or other vegetable oil*
3 *pounds lean beef, cut into very small cubes*
3 *garlic cloves, chopped*
7 *medium ripe tomatoes, chopped*
2 *teaspoons chopped fresh oregano*
5 *teaspoons chili powder*
2 *teaspoons paprika*
3 *jalapeños, chopped, including seeds*
1 *tablespoon cumin*
2 *teaspoons salt*
3 *cups cooked rice*

1. In a Dutch oven, sauté the onion in the oil. Add the beef and cook until it begins to brown, stirring constantly.

2. Add the garlic and tomatoes, stirring to combine. Next, add the oregano, chili powder, paprika, jalapeños, cumin, and salt.
3. Bring just to a boil, stirring to be sure the mixture doesn't stick. Turn the heat down and simmer for 2 or 3 hours, stirring occasionally. Serve in preheated bowls over about ¼ cup rice per person.

10 SERVINGS

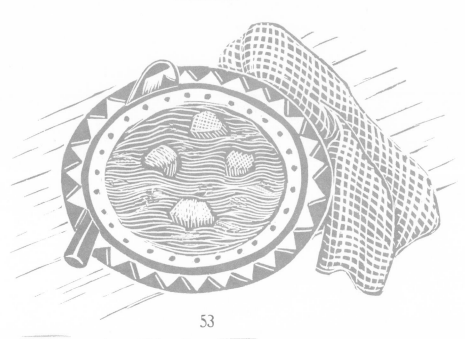

Green Tomato Crisp with Rosemary

You can serve tomatoes with every course, from appetizer to soup to entrée to dessert. And not just one dessert. There are cakes, green tomato pies, green tomato mincemeat pies, and this crunchy delight.

1   tablespoon olive or other vegetable oil
5   large green tomatoes
½   cup plus 2 tablespoons butter
½   teaspoon ginger
1   teaspoon cinnamon
¼   teaspoon nutmeg
1   tablespoon finely chopped fresh rosemary
Zest of 1 large lemon
1   cup dark brown sugar
1   cup unflavored bread crumbs
1   cup wheat germ
Juice of 1 large lemon

1. Preheat the oven to 350°F and lightly oil a covered baking dish.
2. Wash the tomatoes and chop coarsely. Melt 2 tablespoons of the butter in a large saucepan and add the tomatoes, spices, rosemary, and lemon zest. Add the brown sugar and stir well.

3. In a smaller pan, melt the remaining ½ cup butter and add the bread crumbs and wheat germ.
4. Put half the crumb mixture in the baking dish, add the tomato mixture, and squeeze the lemon juice over it. Spread the rest of the crumb mixture over the top, cover, and bake 35 minutes. Remove the cover and bake another 10 minutes. Serve warm.

6 SERVINGS

PEPPERS
LOVE
HERBS

Garlicky Bean and Pepper Dip

Refried beans have become a great favorite for hors d'oeuvres. Here's a nonfried bean dip with garlic and cilantro that packs a punch. Remember to handle the jalapeños like the tigers they are.

>   2 tablespoons extra virgin olive oil
>   2 fresh jalapeño peppers, cored, seeded, and minced
>   1 small onion, minced
>   2 garlic cloves, chopped
>   1 can (8-ounce) black beans, drained
>   1 large sweet green pepper, cored, seeded, and chopped
>   2 tablespoons minced fresh cilantro

1. In the order listed, put the olive oil, jalapeños, onion, garlic, black beans, and sweet pepper in a blender or food processor and purée.
2. Pour into a bowl, stir in the cilantro, cover tightly with plastic wrap, and refrigerate for at least 1 hour to allow flavors to blend. Remove 15 minutes before serving. Serve with tortilla chips, corn chips, or celery stalks.

1½ CUPS

Roasted Pepper and Cilantro Butter

For a different spread on crackers — perhaps even crackers you've made yourself — try this pretty butter.

> 4 tablespoons butter, at room temperature
> ½ cup roasted peppers (see instructions, page 95)
> 2 teaspoons hot mustard
> 3 teaspoons chopped fresh cilantro
> Salt and freshly ground pepper

1. In a food processor or blender, cream the butter and gradually add the roasted peppers through the top while it is running.
2. When the butter is rosy red, stop the machine and scrape the sides. Add the mustard and cilantro, process until mixed, and season with salt and pepper to taste.
3. Serve at room temperature.

½ CUP

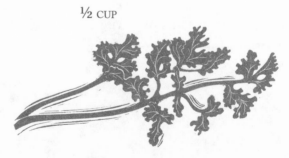

Red Pepper and Garlic Spread

This garlicky spread can go on crackers, chips, crisp slices of cucumber or zucchini, or rounds of rye bread. But it's best on crostini — thin slices of crusty French bread that you brush on both sides with olive oil and then bake in a hot oven (400°F) for 10 minutes or less.

 3 *sweet red peppers, roasted and peeled*
 ½ *cup extra virgin olive oil*
 ¼ *cup pitted and chopped black olives*
 6 *garlic cloves, minced or crushed*
 2 *tablespoons capers*
 1 *tablespoon minced fresh parsley*
 2 *teaspoons lemon juice*
 Salt and freshly ground black pepper

1. Roast the peppers under the broiler until they are partly charred; place in a plastic bag for 10 minutes. Then peel and dice them.
2. Start with the olive oil, and then add the peppers, olives, garlic, capers, parsley, and lemon juice into a blender or food processor and process for a short time. The mixture should be coarse, not puréed.
3. Let stand at room temperature for at least 1 hour before serving to allow flavors to blend. Add salt and pepper to taste.

2 CUPS

Chili and Cilantro Sambal

For this Indian-style dish, to be used as a condiment with cold meats or with curry, try those green chili peppers that look like a witch's finger — long, curved, and talonlike. Respect their hotness. Using a melon baller is a good way to remove the seeds. If you have a pioneer spirit, spread this sambal on a turkey or cheese sandwich.

> 6 *fresh green chili peppers, cored, seeded, and minced*
> 1 *cup fresh cilantro*
> ¼ *cup fresh chives*
> 1½ *slices whole wheat bread, broken into pieces*
> ¼ *cup lime juice*
> ⅓ *cup extra virgin olive oil*
> ½ *inch fresh gingerroot, peeled and minced*
> ½ *teaspoon cumin*
> *Salt*

1. Combine chilis, cilantro, chives, bread, lime juice, olive oil, gingerroot, and cumin in a food processor or blender and pulse until the ingredients have combined but still have texture.
2. Season with salt to taste, and refrigerate for several hours to allow flavors to blend. Serve at room temperature.

1 CUP

Green Pepper Jelly with Oregano

Some like it hot, some like it mild — with peppers, you can have it your way. And, in fact, if the garden or the roadside stand features more sweet red peppers than green ones, use half and half for a red and green pepper jelly.

> 2 cups ground sweet green peppers
> 1 hot pepper (optional)
> 1 tablespoon minced fresh oregano
> I cup white vinegar
> 1 box powdered pectin
> 3½ cups sugar

1. Finely grind the peppers in a hand grinder or food processor.
2. Mix peppers, oregano, vinegar, and pectin in a saucepan and bring to a rolling boil, the kind you can't stir down.
3. Add the sugar and boil hard for 3 minutes, stirring constantly.
4. Pour into clean, hot jelly jars with two-part canning lids, leaving ¼ inch of headroom.
5. Process in boiling water bath for 5 minutes.

4 HALF PINTS

Pepper Thyme Cheese Bread

You can have your peppers toasted for breakfast, too, with the sweetness of honey and the fragrance of thyme. And if you want to try just a hint of hot, add four or five drops of chili oil to the dough, along with the honey.

2 tablespoons dry yeast

2 tablespoons plus 1 teaspoon honey

4–5 drops chili oil, optional

½ cup lukewarm water

3 tablespoons extra virgin olive oil

1 sweet green pepper, finely chopped

1 sweet red pepper, finely chopped

1 cup milk

1½ teaspoons salt

2 tablespoons minced fresh thyme

3 ounces Monterey Jack cheese, shredded (¾ cup)

3 ounces sharp cheddar cheese, shredded (¾ cup)

2 eggs, beaten, plus 1 egg, beaten

4–4½ cups all-purpose unbleached flour

½ cup wheat bran

1. Combine the yeast, 1 teaspoon of the honey, the chili oil if using, and the water in a small bowl and set aside until the yeast foams.
2. In a medium skillet, heat 1 tablespoon of the olive oil and sauté the peppers until they are limp, 3 to 5 minutes.
3. In a saucepan, combine the milk, the remaining olive oil, and honey. Add the salt, thyme, and cheeses and heat to lukewarm.
4. In a large bowl, combine the peppers, 2 of the beaten eggs, the yeast mixture, and the milk mixture. Stir in 2 cups of the flour. Add the wheat bran and enough additional flour so that the dough begins to pull away from the sides of the bowl.
5. Cover and let the dough rise for 30 minutes. If your house is cold and the dough is sluggish, put a heating pad under it on low or medium. It will perk up.
6. Punch down the dough, divide it in half, and shape each half into a loaf to fit a greased 9-inch loaf pan. Let the bread rise another 30 minutes.
7. Preheat the oven to 375°F. Brush the top of each loaf with the remaining beaten egg, and bake for 30 to 35 minutes.

2 LOAVES

Cornbread with Jalapeños

You can substitute any variety of hot pepper for the jalapeño in this recipe, or change the amount to suit your taste. Handle hot peppers with care: If you get hot pepper juice on your hands and then rub an eye, flush it out with copious amounts of water. The better course is to wear rubber gloves and wash utensils and cutting boards after dealing with these peppers.

½ cup fresh corn kernels or dry-packed canned corn
½ teaspoon salt
1¼ cups low-fat yogurt
½ cup butter, melted, plus more for greasing pan
2 eggs, beaten, or ½ cup cholesterol-free egg substitute
3 tablespoons chopped fresh oregano
3 teaspoons baking powder
1 cup yellow cornmeal
¼ teaspoon white pepper
¼ pound cheddar cheese, shredded
1 jalapeño pepper, cored, seeded, and minced

1. Preheat the oven to 350°F and butter a 2½-quart casserole dish.
2. In a large bowl, combine the corn kernels, salt, yogurt, melted butter, and eggs or egg product.
3. Combine the oregano, baking powder, cornmeal, and white pepper and stir into the corn and yogurt mixture. Chop the shredded cheese into smaller pieces and fold into the mixture. Add the jalapeño.
4. Pour the batter into the baking dish and bake for 1 hour. Serve with plenty of butter.

8 SQUARES

Savory Red Pepper Chowder

You've had chowder with clams, chowder with onions, chowder with fish, and chowder with corn. It's time for chowder with savory and sweet red peppers, picked when they've just turned glossy red and are still crisp.

4 tablespoons butter
2 medium onions, chopped
1 garlic clove, chopped
1 tablespoon minced fresh savory
1 bay leaf, ground with mortar and pestle
½ cup chopped button mushrooms
4 sweet red peppers (3 cups chopped)
Juice of ½ lemon
2 cups chicken broth
3 large potatoes, or enough for 1 cup thinly sliced
4 cups low-fat milk
Salt and freshly ground pepper
¼ cup coarsely chopped fresh parsley

1. In a soup pot, melt the butter and cook the onions gently until they are soft and golden, not browned. After the first 5 minutes, add the garlic, savory, and bay leaf, along with the mushrooms, chopped peppers, and lemon juice. Cook another 5 minutes.

2. Add the broth and sliced potatoes. Simmer, covered, for 25 minutes, or until the potatoes are tender.
3. Add the milk, stir well, and reheat. Add salt and pepper to taste and serve, garnishing with the chopped parsley.

2 QUARTS

Albuquerque Chili with Oregano

Chili con carne, it's called in Mexico; in the United States, the title is more likely to include a hint of fire. Steaming bowls of chili are two-alarm (a little hot), three-alarm (hotter), or four-alarm (conflagration). This one has enough hot chili peppers in it to put it in the four-alarm category for most firefighters.

¼ cup extra virgin olive oil
2 pounds lean beef, cut into ½-inch cubes
2 tablespoons all-purpose unbleached flour
1 medium yellow onion, chopped
2 garlic cloves, chopped
3 large ripe tomatoes, chopped
6–8 small mild chili peppers, seeded and thinly sliced
3 small hot red chili peppers, seeded and thinly sliced,
    or 1 habanero pepper
4 teaspoons minced fresh oregano
½ teaspoon cumin seed
2 cups beef broth
Salt and freshly ground black pepper
4 cups cooked rice

1. In a large skillet, heat 2 tablespoons of the oil and brown the beef. Drain off the fat. Place the beef in a large soup pot.
2. In the same skillet, heat the rest of the oil and blend in the flour, onion, and garlic. Cook until the onion is just starting to brown.
3. Add the onion mixture, tomatoes, chili peppers, oregano, cumin seed, and beef broth to the soup pot. Simmer, covered, for 2 hours, stirring occasionally.
4. Add salt and pepper to taste. Serve in warmed chili bowls over rice or with rice on the side.

4 SERVINGS

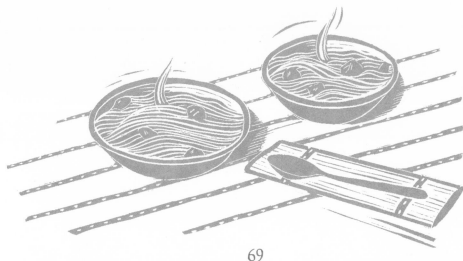

Red Pepper Quiche

Even though it's ubiquitous, quiche still sounds exotic, elegant — like something that could be described in the J. Peterman catalog. This quiche is herbed and handsome to boot. What more could you ask of eggs in a pie shell?

1 *tablespoon extra virgin olive oil*
1 *sweet red pepper, finely chopped*
8 *slices bacon*
6 *ounces Gruyère cheese, finely shredded (1½ cups)*
9-inch unbaked pie shell
3 *eggs*
1 *cup light cream*
½ *cup low-fat milk*
1 *tablespoon snipped fresh chives*
1 *teaspoon minced fresh chervil*
Salt and freshly ground pepper
Dash of cayenne

1. In a small skillet, heat the olive oil and gently sauté the chopped pepper until it is soft but not browned. In a microwave, cook the bacon between double layers of paper towels for 5 minutes. Change the towels and cook another 2 minutes if bacon isn't crisp. (Or you can cook the bacon the conventional way, in a skillet.) When the bacon slices are no longer hot, crumble them.
2. Preheat the oven to 375°F. Sprinkle the shredded cheese, crumbled bacon, and red pepper evenly over the pie shell.
3. Beat the eggs, cream, and milk until frothy. Add the chives, chervil, salt and pepper to taste, and cayenne, and whisk well. Pour into pie shell.
4. Bake for 45 minutes or until the quiche is firm and browned. Serve in warm wedges.

6 SERVINGS

*The light purple flowers of chives
make a flavorful addition to salads.*

Pepper Frittata with Dill

Fresh egg whites make not only a satisfying omelette but also a delicious frittata. For brunch, a frittata is more spectacular than scrambled eggs or omelettes. Garlic and dill add zing.

1 tablespoon butter
1 cup chopped onions
1 sweet green pepper, finely chopped
1 sweet red pepper, finely chopped
1 tablespoon snipped fresh dill
2 garlic cloves, minced
Salt and white pepper
6 egg whites
3 slices low-fat cheese, shredded

1. Preheat the broiler in the oven. In a large skillet, melt the butter and slowly cook the onions until they begin to soften, about 10 minutes.
2. Add the peppers, dill, garlic, and salt and pepper to taste to the pan and cook another 5 minutes.
3. In a bowl, beat the egg whites until they are foamy and nearly stiff.

4. Pour the whites over the vegetable mixture, lifting the vegetables so the egg can run underneath. Cook on low heat for 3 to 4 minutes.
5. Place the shredded cheese on top and put the skillet under the broiler for 2 minutes, or until the cheese melts and starts to turn brown.

2–3 SERVINGS

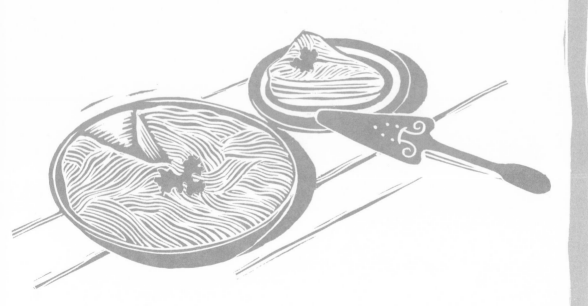

Peter Piper's Dill Peppers

If Peter Piper had picked these peppers, he would have gone back for more and more and more. They're sweet. But they're sour. And they're made the day before they're served, so they're easy on the cook.

2 sweet yellow peppers
2 sweet green peppers
1 long English-style cucumber, or 2 regular size
6 young carrots
3 scallions
2 teaspoons salt
4 tablespoons sugar
4 tablespoons white wine vinegar
3 tablespoons snipped fresh dill

1. Slit the peppers lengthwise into strips as thin as possible. If the peppers are very large, cut the strips in half.
2. Cut the cucumber in half lengthwise, remove the seeds with a teaspoon or melon baller, and slice into ¼-inch chunks.
3. Peel the carrots and slice into thin circles.
4. Cut the scallions lengthwise and shred as finely as possible into 2-inch lengths.

5. Put the peppers, cucumber, carrots, and scallions into a large glass bowl and sprinkle the salt over them. Mix and let stand, unrefrigerated, for 3 hours. Drain off the water that is drawn out by the salt.
6. Whisk the sugar and vinegar together. Sprinkle the dill over the salad, add the sugar and vinegar mixture, and toss gently until the dressing is thoroughly mixed through the vegetables. Cover tightly with plastic wrap and refrigerate overnight. Serve chilled.

10 SERVINGS

Parsleyed Pepper Pyramid Salad

When peppers are plentiful locally, they make an affordable and handsome salad. In the winter, splurge on those giants from Holland — why doesn't anyone grow them in this country? — and perk up the table with this structure.

2 *large sweet green peppers*
1 *large sweet red pepper*
1 *large sweet yellow or orange pepper*
1 *red onion*
Juice of ½ lemon
4 *tablespoons olive oil*
⅛ *teaspoon cayenne*
1 *teaspoon cumin*
Large bunch of light-green oak-leaf lettuce,
      or 3 heads bibb lettuce
12–15 *pitted black olives*
Freshly ground black pepper
¼ *cup chopped fresh parsley*

1. Leaving the cores in for stability, slice the 4 peppers into thin rings, trying not to break any of them. Discard the core end.
2. Slice the onion thinly.
3. Whisk together the lemon juice, oil, cayenne, and cumin.

4. Mound the lettuce leaves on a large glass plate, piling them higher in the center. Circle the outside of the plate with a row of onion slices. Place green pepper rings on top of the onions, followed by a row of red pepper rings slightly overlapping the green ones. Working toward the center, add another row of green rings, then a row of the yellow or orange, then another red. Repeat, with the circles getting smaller and smaller, until you have used up the peppers and created a pyramid of salad.
5. Arrange the black olives on the salad. Pour the dressing over the top, grind black pepper to taste over the pyramid, and sprinkle with the parsley.

6 SERVINGS

Arranged Pepper Salad

Chinese and Japanese dishes are often tossed in a wok, but other times the various ingredients are carefully arranged as if they were flowers or sweets. This salad tastes good and also looks beautiful. Triple it to make it an edible decoration on a buffet.

> 2 *tablespoons light soy sauce*
> 1 *teaspoon sugar*
> 1 *garlic clove, pressed*
> 2 *tablespoons chopped fresh chervil*
> 5 *tablespoons extra virgin olive oil*
> 2 *tablespoons white wine vinegar*
> 1 *cup torn leaf lettuce*
> ½ *cup torn spinach leaves*
> ½ *cup finely shredded cabbage*
> 1 *cup fresh bean sprouts*
> 1 *cup thinly sliced button mushrooms*
> 1 *sweet green pepper, sliced in thin strips*
> 1 *sweet banana pepper, or other yellow pepper,*
>   *sliced in thin strips*

1. Whisk together the soy sauce, sugar, garlic clove, chervil, olive oil, and vinegar. Set aside so the flavors have a chance to blend.

2. Toss the lettuce, spinach, and cabbage together and circle the outside of a shallow bowl with the mixture.
3. Mound the bean sprouts in the center and arrange the mushroom slices around them, overlapping each slice with the next. Make decorative X's with green and yellow pepper strips on the bean sprouts.
4. Drizzle the dressing over all.

4 SERVINGS

Grilled Salad with Herbs

Here's a salad that can be served warm, not-so-warm, or even chilled if you want to wait awhile. While grilling lamb chops or chicken, add some vegetables to the fire: red, green, and yellow peppers, a small eggplant — or whatever is available — Spanish onions, a couple of leeks.

1 *sweet red pepper*
1 *sweet green pepper*
1 *sweet yellow pepper*
1 *small eggplant*
1 *Spanish onion*
2 *large leeks, split lengthwise and rinsed carefully*
2 *garlic cloves, minced*
1 *tablespoon chopped fresh oregano*
1 *tablespoon chopped fresh parsley*
1½ *tablespoons balsamic vinegar*
¼ *cup extra virgin olive oil*
½ *teaspoon dry mustard*
Salt and freshly ground pepper
12 *cherry tomatoes*

1. Put the peppers, eggplant, onion, and leeks on the grill and let them cook until charred, turning occasionally. You may need a piece of screening or a slab of slate over the grate so the vegetables won't fall into the fire.
2. While the vegetables are cooking, combine the garlic, oregano, parsley, vinegar, oil, dry mustard, and salt and pepper to taste in a jar with a tightly fitting lid. Shake well and set aside to let the flavors blend.
3. When the vegetables are well cooked, remove from the grill, peel, and chop coarsely. Place in an attractive salad bowl and either chill for 1 hour or serve warm with the dressing. Garnish with the tomatoes.

4 TO 6 SERVINGS

Herbed Peppers and Oranges

Human minds are filled with color codes, so color — consciously or unconsciously — affects how people feel about food. That's why you just can't plop a chicken breast, a mound of mashed potatoes, and a pile of cauliflower on a plate. This salad, for color and taste, is an attention getter.

3 sweet green peppers, cored and seeded
2 oranges, with the zest removed from one and reserved
2 heads Boston or bibb lettuce
4 cups torn spinach leaves, with tough stems removed
3 tablespoons extra virgin olive oil
1 tablespoon balsamic vinegar
2 teaspoons lemon verbena, minced
¼ teaspoon sugar
Zest of 1 orange
Salt and freshly ground black pepper
1 red onion, sliced in paper-thin rings
¼ cup farmer cheese

1. Slice the peppers into long thin strips. Cut the oranges in half, as you would a grapefruit, and scoop out the sections with a grapefruit spoon.

2. Toss the lettuce and spinach together and mound on a large white or clear-glass plate.
3. Make the dressing, whisking together the oil, vinegar, lemon verbena, sugar, orange zest, and salt and pepper to taste.
4. Arrange the pepper slices, orange sections, and onion rings on top of the lettuce in a decorative way. Scatter crumbled farmer cheese over the top and drizzle the dressing over the whole salad.

6 SERVINGS

83

Savory Shrimp and Pepper Salad

Summertime, and the living is supposed to be easier. Take some garden peppers and onions and herbs, cook up some shrimp and pasta, and have dinner ready before lunch and the heat of the day.

½ pound rotini or elbow pasta
1 cup water
Juice of 1 lemon
1 pound uncooked shrimp
1 large sweet red or orange pepper, chopped
1 tablespoon minced red onion
2 tablespoons minced fresh parsley
4 tablespoons crumbled feta cheese
½ cup extra virgin olive oil
1 tablespoon Balsamic vinegar
1 garlic clove, minced
1 tablespoon minced fresh savory
¼ teaspoon white pepper
Salt

1. In a large saucepan, bring 4 quarts of water to a boil and cook the pasta until it is just tender. Drain, flush with cold water, and drain again.
2. In a saucepan, bring the water and 1 tablespoon of the lemon juice to a boil. Add the shrimp and simmer for 3 to 5 minutes. Drain, shell, and devein.
3. Combine the pasta, shrimp, pepper, onion, parsley, and feta cheese in a large salad bowl.
4. Combine the oil, vinegar, garlic, savory, pepper, and salt to taste in a jar with a tightly fitting lid, and shake to blend. Pour over the salad and toss to coat. Chill for at least 1 hour before serving.

SERVES 4–6

Steamed Peppers with Black Olives

Most pepper recipes find the peppers surrounded by other vegetables or meats. This one surrounds them with fresh herbs to let the peppers shine.

2 *large sweet green peppers*
2 *large sweet red or orange peppers*
3 *tablespoons extra virgin olive oil*
2 *garlic cloves, minced or pressed*
2 *onions, minced*
1 *tablespoon finely chopped fresh, oregano*
1 *tablespoon finely chopped fresh, parsley*
1 *teaspoon finely chopped fresh, rosemary*
1½ *teaspoons ground cumin*
½ *jalapeño pepper, cored, seeded, and minced*
Salt and freshly ground pepper
12 *pitted black olives, coarsely chopped*
1 *tablespoon capers*

1. Wash the peppers, pat them dry, and cut them in half. Remove the seeds and membranes and slice lengthwise into 6 strips per pepper.
2. In a large skillet, heat the oil and add the pepper strips, skin side down.

3. Sprinkle the garlic and onions over the top, then the oregano, parsley, rosemary, cumin, jalapeño, and salt and pepper to taste. Toss and stir to lightly coat everything with the oil, adding another teaspoon or two of oil if necessary.

4. Cover and cook over medium heat until the onions and peppers are tender but not mushy, about 15 minutes. Add the black olives and capers and toss again. Cook another 5 minutes without covering.

8 SERVINGS

Stir-Fried Peppers with Parsley

The Chinese get the wok very hot, add a small amount of oil, then put in various flavorings and the freshest of vegetables and toss them about rapidly for a very short time. The result comes in way ahead of boiling.

1 tablespoon cornstarch
1 tablespoon cold water
2 tablespoons peanut oil
1 tablespoon sesame seed oil
2 tablespoons shredded hot red pepper
1 tablespoon black bean sauce
3 garlic cloves, minced
2 large sweet green peppers, cored, seeded, and cut
    into ¼-inch strips
4 large carrots, peeled and shredded
¼ pound fresh bean sprouts
¼ cup chicken broth
¼ cup sherry or rice wine
3 scallions, green and white parts, shredded
¼ cup chopped fresh parsley

88

1. Dissolve the cornstarch in the water and set aside.
2. Heat a wok or large skillet until a drop of water skitters around the pan. Add the peanut and sesame oils and swirl to coat the pan. Stir in the hot pepper, black bean sauce, and garlic. Scoop and turn the mixture for 1 minute.
3. Add the sweet peppers, carrots, and bean sprouts, continuing to scoop and turn the vegetables rapidly for about 1 minute. Stir in the chicken broth and sherry or wine, and heat to boiling.
4. Stir in the cornstarch mixture and stir about 20 seconds or until thickened. Add the scallions and parsley. Cook and stir for 30 seconds. Serve as hot as possible.

4–6 SERVINGS

Potatoes and Peppers

Basically, these potatoes and peppers are steamed. The potatoes may get a little brown, but it's fine if they stay white. The object is to cook them so slowly that they get soft gradually and absorb the taste of onions, garlic, and peppers. An electric skillet works well for this dish because the heat can be regulated precisely.

10 *large potatoes*
 5 *tablespoons extra virgin olive oil*
 1 *onion, finely chopped*
 5 *garlic cloves, chopped*
 2 *large sweet green peppers,*
   chopped
½ *cup chopped fresh parsley*

1. Peel the potatoes, cut into ½-inch cubes, and leave in cold water until it is time to cook them.
2. In a deep skillet that has a cover, heat the oil and cook the onion and garlic slowly for about 5 minutes. Add the peppers. Drain the potatoes and add them. Stir.
3. Turn the heat almost to low and cook 1–1½ hours. A few minutes before serving, stir in the chopped parsley.

8–10 SERVINGS

Almond Pepper Sauce

A Spanish sauce made with some sweet and some hot peppers can be used on fresh grilled tuna steaks or swordfish or on steamed vegetables. A tablespoonful or two could easily be added to a seafood soup or stew.

1 cup blanched, slivered almonds
2 hard-cooked egg yolks
1 sweet red pepper, roasted, peeled, cored, and seeded
1 fresh habanero or other hot red pepper
2 garlic cloves, chopped
¼ cup chopped fresh parsley
1 tablespoon chopped fresh cilantro
¼ cup white wine vinegar
¾ cup extra virgin olive oil
3 tablespoons boiling water

1. Combine almonds, egg yolks, sweet and hot peppers, garlic, parsley, cilantro, and vinegar in a food processor or blender. Process until smooth.
2. With the machine running, slowly add the olive oil and then the boiling water. Store in a glass container and refrigerate until needed.

2 CUPS

Peppers Stuffed with Herbed Cheese

Even if you're a dedicated carnivore, you can make a meal out of these hearty cheese-crammed peppers. Try them hot with an all-green salad with citrus dressing on the side. They can be made with red, green, or orange peppers.

4 large sweet peppers
1 large tomato, peeled
1 tablespoon chopped fresh basil
1 teaspoon snipped fresh chives
½ teaspoon Worcestershire sauce
Salt and white pepper
½ pound sharp cheddar cheese cut into ¼-inch cubes
½ pound Swiss cheese, cut into ¼-inch cubes

1. Preheat the oven to 375°F, and grease a baking dish large enough to hold the peppers upright.
2. Slice the stem end off the peppers and carefully remove the seeds and membranes.
3. Bring about 2 inches of water to a boil in a large kettle, stand the peppers in the kettle, and cook for about 6 minutes.
4. Remove the peppers and place in the baking dish. Drop the tomato into the hot water for 30 seconds, remove, peel, and chop.

5. Combine the tomato, basil, chives, Worcestershire sauce, and salt and pepper to taste, then spoon into the peppers.
6. Mix the two cheeses together and add to the peppers, rounding off the tops. The peppers should be stuffed full.
7. Bake for at least 20 minutes, until the peppers are hot and the cheese is melted.

SERVES 4

Dilly Yellow Peppers and Beans

Put olives, garlic, and anchovies together, and you start thinking of the south of France, where vegetables reign supreme. If you can't find yellow peppers, use red. If you can't find red, use green.

4 sweet yellow peppers, sliced
   lengthwise and seeded
2 tablespoons extra virgin olive oil
1 yellow onion, finely chopped
3 garlic cloves, minced
¼ cup chopped fresh parsley

2 tablespoons snipped fresh dill
1 can (16-ounce) black beans
1 can anchovies, drained and mashed
¼ cup dry white wine
12–15 Greek olives, pitted and chopped
   Freshly ground black pepper

1. Blanch the pepper halves in boiling water for 3 to 5 minutes. Drain, run cool water over the peppers, and drain again.
2. In a medium-size skillet, heat the oil and cook the onion for 5 minutes. Add the garlic and cook another 5 minutes or until the onion is translucent but not browned. Stir in the parsley and dill.
3. Preheat the oven to 350°F. Transfer the onion mixture to a bowl. Add the black beans, anchovies, wine, olives, and black pepper to taste. Fill the pepper halves with the mixture and place them in a baking dish with about 3 tablespoons of water in the bottom. Cover and bake for 20 minutes.

4–6 SERVINGS

Red Pepper Sauce with Fish

Roasted peppers are a simple dish — and a delicacy. After roasting, a pepper can be used in any number of ways. Here, roasted peppers blended with basil and parsley become a sauce for fish.

4 small sweet red peppers	2 tablespoons chopped fresh parsley
1 cup chicken broth	½ teaspoon turmeric
½ cup dry white wine	1 tablespoon butter
1 garlic clove, minced	Grilled or poached fish
1 tablespoon chopped fresh basil	Lemon wedges

1. To roast peppers, place them in a baking dish and bake uncovered on the lowest rack in the oven at 450°F for 30 minutes or until they are blackened on all sides. Turn 3 or 4 times during the roasting.
   When they are done, place them in a paper bag and roll the top closed. Leave for 10 minutes. Take them out and peel.
2. Put peeled peppers, broth, wine, and garlic in a blender and purée.
3. Pour the mixture into a medium skillet; add the basil, parsley, and turmeric and cook slowly until the sauce has thickened. Add the butter and reheat until the butter is melted. Make a circle of sauce on each individual plate and place a piece of grilled or poached fish on it. Top with a lemon wedge for garnish.

ABOUT 1 CUP

Herbed Pepper Calzones

Basically, a calzone is a cross between a folded-up pizza and a turnover. If you've never had one, this mix of peppers, herbs, and cheese is a good place to start.

1 tablespoon yeast	2 teaspoons minced fresh thyme
1⅓ cups warm water	3 sweet green peppers, cored, seeded,
2 tablespoons canola oil	and sliced into thin strips
Pinch of sugar	3–5 tablespoons olive oil
1 teaspoon salt	2 cups chopped shiitake mushrooms
4 cups all-purpose unbleached flour	½ cup chopped black olives
3 Italian hot sausages	1½ cups shredded mozzarella cheese
3 sweet turkey sausages	¼ cup grated Parmesan cheese
2 large onions, diced	¼ cup grated Romano cheese
1 garlic clove, minced	1 egg
1 tablespoon minced fresh marjoram	4 cups heated tomato sauce (optional)

1. Combine the yeast, water, canola oil, and sugar in a bowl and let stand until the yeast foams. Add the salt and 2 cups of the flour and beat the dough until it is elastic and smooth. Stir in the remaining 2 cups of flour.

2. Knead the dough for about 10 minutes, adding flour if necessary. Cover with a damp towel or plastic wrap and set in a warm place for about 45 minutes. It should double in size.

3. Remove the casings from both kinds of sausages, then crumble the sausage into a large skillet. Fry, continuing to break up the sausage into fine pieces. Remove the meat to a large bowl, drain off all but 2 tablespoons of the fat, and add the onions, garlic, marjoram, thyme, and peppers. If there is no fat, add 2 tablespoons of the olive oil.

4. Cook the onions and peppers until soft and add to the sausage. Heat 3 tablespoons of olive oil in the same pan and cook the mushrooms until they are soft, about 5 minutes. Add them to the vegetables and sausage. Stir in the cheeses.

5. Preheat the oven to 375°F and grease a cookie sheet.

6. When the dough has risen, punch it down and divide into 8 chunks. Form each chunk into a ball and, on a lightly floured board, roll each into an 8-inch circle. Spoon ⅛ of the filling onto each circle, brush the edges of the dough with water, fold in half, and crimp the edges.

7. Place the calzones on the cookie sheet and let rise, covered with a damp towel, for about 20 minutes. Beat the egg and brush it on the top of the calzones. Bake for 35 minutes. Serve hot as is or with tomato sauce.

8 SERVINGS

Peppers and Sun-Dried Tomatoes with Pasta

Pasta, homemade or store-bought, is always available. When vegetables are at their prime, they toss well with pasta — any or all of them. Try this one with sweet peppers, hot sausage, and herbs, a sort of distant cousin of carbonara. Eat it with spaghetti or linguini.

> 4 *sweet red bell peppers*
> 4 *tablespoons olive oil*
> 2 *Italian sausages, hot or sweet*
> 4 *garlic cloves, peeled and sliced in half*
> 1 *pound spaghetti or linguini*
> 2 *tablespoons sun-dried tomatoes packed in oil, drained and chopped*
> 3 *tablespoons grated Romano cheese*
> ¾ *cup grated Parmesan cheese*
> 3 *tablespoons chopped fresh basil*
> 3 *tablespoons chopped fresh parsley*
> 2 *scallions, green and white parts, shredded*

1. Roast the peppers in a baking pan, uncovered, on the lowest rack in the oven at 450°F for about 30 minutes or until they are blackened on all sides.

Turn 3 or 4 times during the roasting. When they are done, place them in a paper bag and roll the top closed. Leave for 10 minutes. When you take them out, peel and let cool. Chop them coarsely.

2. In a skillet, heat the oil. Remove the casings from the sausages and crumble the sausages into the pan. Add the garlic and cook, continuing to separate the sausage meat into crumb-size pieces until they are brown and crisp. Remove the garlic and discard.

3. In the meantime, bring a large pot of water to a boil and cook the spaghetti or liguini.

4. Combine the warm peppers, sausage, and sun-dried tomatoes. In a separate bowl, combine the Romano and ½ cup of the Parmesan with the basil, parsley, and scallions. When the pasta is cooked, drain it quickly and place in a large pasta bowl. Cover with the pepper mixture, then the cheese and herb mixture, and toss. Serve at once with the remaining cheese.

4 SERVINGS

Tarragon Chicken and Sweet Peppers

Certain baseball players, heart patients, semivegetarians, and the cholesterol conscious all have a basic fear: They eat so much chicken every year that they're afraid they may wake up squawking one morning. Perhaps they will, but they don't need to be bored. Chicken can be made more ways than there are days in the year, enhanced by almost any herb in the garden.

> 3 chicken breasts, boned, skinned, and halved
> ¼ cup unbleached flour
> 2 tablespoons minced fresh tarragon
> Salt and freshly ground pepper
> 3 tablespoons extra virgin olive oil
> 1 large sweet onion, diced
> 2 sweet green peppers, cored, seeded, and cut in strips
> 1 cup dry white wine
> 1 tablespoon soy sauce
> 1 cup seedless white grapes

1. Pound the chicken breasts between layers of wax paper until they are fairly thin. Dredge the chicken breasts in the flour, tarragon, and salt and pepper to taste.

2. Heat the oil in a large skillet and add the chicken, turning quickly to brown on both sides. Remove the chicken with a Chinese strainer or slotted spoon and place in a shallow baking dish.
3. Preheat the oven to 375°F. Add the onion and peppers to the skillet and cook slowly until tender. Add the wine and soy sauce, heat to boiling, and cook for another minute. Pour the sauce over the chicken. Cover the baking dish and bake for 12 minutes.
4. In the meantime, slice the grapes in half. When the chicken is ready, add the grapes and bake another 5 to 6 minutes.

4–6 SERVINGS

Stuffed Peppers with Basil

When the sweet green peppers are fat, juicy, and still crisp, find eight that will make nice boats when they're sliced in half lengthwise. These are just right for stuffing, and half the batch can be frozen for another day. Hint: Watch out for the chili powder — it likes to stick to the pan.

1 pound very lean ground beef
2 large onions, chopped
1 garlic clove, minced
2 tablespoons chopped fresh basil
1 jalapeño pepper, seeded and minced
2 teaspoons chili powder
Salt and freshly ground black pepper
2 cups tomato purée
2 tablespoons sugar
1 tablespoon soy sauce
¼ cup low-fat milk
½ pound sharp cheddar cheese, shredded
1½ cups cooked rice
¼ cup chopped fresh parsley
8 sweet green peppers

1. In a large skillet or saucepan, cook the beef, onions, and garlic until the meat is browned.
2. Add the basil, jalapeño pepper, chili powder, and salt and pepper to taste, stirring well. Combine the tomato purée, sugar, soy sauce, and milk and add to the skillet. Bring to a simmer, cover, and cook for 10 minutes.
3. Stir in the shredded cheese and cook over low heat, stirring until the cheese has melted. Stir in the rice and parsley and remove from heat. Set aside to cool.
4. Preheat the oven to 400°F. Bring to a boil in a large pot enough water to cover the peppers. Cut the peppers lengthwise, removing the seeds, stems, and the membranes. Drop into boiling water for about 3 minutes. Drain and cool.
5. Stuff the peppers with the rice mixture. Place peppers on a cookie sheet or in a shallow baking dish. Cover and bake for 30 minutes.
6. To freeze, place peppers on a cookie sheet and put them in the freezer. When they are frozen, wrap, seal, label, and store them in the freezer. To serve from the freezer, partially thaw the peppers in the refrigerator and bake for 45 minutes.

8 SERVINGS

Chinese Pepper Beef

Black beans and peppers contribute distinctive flavors to this beef dish, which can be made either in a wok or a large skillet. Like many Chinese recipes, it looks forbidding because it has so many ingredients. But once the cutting and chopping has been done, much of it ahead of time, the cooking time is short.

STIR-FRY INGREDIENTS

1 *pound lean sirloin tips or filet of beef*
2 *sweet green peppers*
1 *sweet red or yellow pepper*
6 *garlic cloves*
3 *scallions*
1 *fresh hot red chili pepper or 3 dried hunan chilies*
1 *teaspoon cornstarch*
6 *tablespoons water*
5 *tablespoons peanut oil*
Salt and freshly ground black pepper
2½ *tablespoons black bean paste*
1 *tablespoon sherry or rice wine*
¼ *cup finely chopped fresh parsley*

MARINADE INGREDIENTS

¼ *teaspoon salt*
¼ *teaspoon sugar*
2 *teaspoons light soy sauce*
¼ *teaspoon freshly ground pepper*
2 *teaspoons sherry*
1½ *teaspoons cornstarch*
3 *tablespoons water*
1 *teaspoon peanut oil*
1 *teaspoon Asian sesame oil*

1. With a sharp knife, slice the beef across the grain into pieces about an inch wide, 1½ inches long and ¼ inch thick. Put into a large glass bowl.

2. To make the marinade, combine the salt, sugar, soy sauce, pepper, and sherry and pour over the meat.

3. Dissolve the cornstarch in the 3 tablespoons of water. Add to the meat mixture gradually while turning the meat. Add the two oils and turn again. Cover tightly and refrigerate for at least 30 minutes and up to 2 hours.

4. In the meantime, core, halve, and seed the sweet green and red peppers and cut them into thin slices, lengthwise. Peel and mince or press the garlic. Clean and cut the scallions into 1-inch pieces, separating the white part from the green. Core, seed, and finely chop the hot pepper, being careful not to get the juice on your hands or in your eyes. In a small bowl, dissolve the cornstarch in the 6 tablespoons of water.

5. When the marinating time is up, heat 1 tablespoon of the peanut oil in a pre-heated skillet or wok, swirl the oil around, add the sweet peppers, and stir-fry for about 2 minutes, keeping the vegetables moving constantly. Season with salt and pepper to taste and remove to a warm plate.

6. Reheat the wok or skillet, add the rest of the oil, and swirl it around. Add the garlic and white part of the scallions. Keep stirring.

7. Add the black bean paste and the hot pepper. Stir in the beef with any remaining marinade and stir and toss until the beef is partially cooked.

8. Splash the sherry into the pan and continue to stir and toss the meat. Add the dissolved cornstarch, sweet peppers, and green part of the scallions. Mix until the sauce has thickened and the beef is done, perhaps another 2 minutes. Serve immediately, garnished with parsley.

2 SERVINGS IF USED ALONE, 4 IF OTHER MAIN DISHES ARE PREPARED

Venison and Peppers with Savory

Our friend Gary doesn't come home from the hunt empty-handed as a rule. So when it's deer season, his success nets a fair amount of venison. This recipe with peppers and savory is a delicious approach, and for those who don't care for venison, it's easy enough to substitute beef.

1 pound of venison round steak or other steak
1 tablespoon cornstarch
1 teaspoon sugar
½ inch gingerroot, peeled and shredded
2–3 tablespoons light soy sauce
1½ tablespoons dry sherry or dandelion wine
2 medium or 3 small sweet green or red peppers
4 tablespoons extra virgin olive oil
½ teaspoon salt
1 garlic clove, crushed
2 tablespoons minced fresh savory
2 cups cooked rice

1. Cut venison across the grain into slices about 2 inches long and ¼ inch thick.
2. Combine cornstarch, sugar, and gingerroot and blend in the soy sauce and sherry or wine. Toss with the sliced venison in a large glass or ceramic bowl and set aside.
3. Cut the peppers into 1½-inch pieces. Pour 2 tablespoons of the oil into a large skillet over high heat. Add the salt, then the peppers, and cook, stirring constantly, until the peppers turn a deeper color, about 1 minute.
4. Remove the peppers, leaving the oil. Add the remaining oil, garlic, and savory and stir in the venison mixture. Cook for 2 minutes or until venison is done.
5. Add the peppers to the pan, mix well, heat through, and serve immediately with rice. Add more sherry or wine if you want more sauce.

4 SERVINGS

Scallopini with Peppers
and Shiitake Mushrooms

The veal must be pale and pounded thin. The peppers should be freshly picked and crisp. The mushrooms should be perky, not tired. With optimal ingredients, this dish will melt in your mouth.

8 veal scallopini, pounded thin
4 tablespoons extra virgin olive oil
¼ cup flour
4 tablespoons butter
2 sweet green peppers, cored, seeded, and sliced into
    very thin strips
8 shiitake mushrooms, cleaned and sliced
¼ cup chopped fresh parsley
2 teaspoons chopped fresh sage
Salt and freshly ground pepper
Juice of 1 lemon
½ cup dry white wine
Rice or pasta

1. If the scallopini are not well pounded, pound them some more between two sheets of wax paper.
2. Heat the oil in a large skillet. Dredge the scallopini in the flour, shaking off the excess, and cook them in a single layer, browning quickly, possibly only 1 minute per side. Remove to a warm platter as they are done.
3. Drain the oil from the pan, but do not clean it. Add the butter, and when it has melted, slowly sauté the peppers and mushrooms. After about 5 minutes, stir in the parsley, sage, and salt and pepper to taste. Add the lemon juice and continue to cook for another 1–2 minutes.
4. Add the scallopini to the skillet and scoop the sauce over them, turning them until they are coated. Add the white wine and continue the slow cooking until peppers, mushrooms, veal, and sauce are hot. Serve immediately with rice or pasta.

6 SERVINGS

Pork and Peppers Oriental

The Chinese are magical with pork in many forms, and this recipe has more than a hint of Asian cuisine in its flavorings. And like many Chinese dishes, it cooks so quickly that it's the perfect answer for a two-career family. Fluffy rice and a tossed salad complete the meal.

2 pounds pork loin, lean and boneless
2 garlic cloves, chopped
¼ cup light soy sauce
2 teaspoons cornstarch
3 tablespoons water
4 tablespoons safflower oil
1 inch gingerroot, peeled and shredded
½ cup chopped fresh parsley
1 tablespoon sesame oil
2 teaspoons rice wine vinegar
2 tablespoons sugar
1 large onion, cut into eighths
1 sweet red pepper, cut into strips
1 sweet yellow pepper, cut into strips
2 sweet green peppers, cut into strips
2 medium hot chili peppers, seeded and chopped

1. Slice the pork into ¼-inch-thick slices, stack several slices at once, and cut into thin strips. In a bowl, combine the strips with the garlic and soy sauce. Dissolve the cornstarch in the water, pour over pork, and toss to coat the pieces. Set aside.
2. In a large skillet, heat the safflower oil until it is quite hot. Remove the pork strips from the marinade (reserving the leftover marinade) and add to the skillet, stirring while the meat browns and cooks, about 5 minutes. Remove the pork to a platter.
3. Add to the bowl with the remaining marinade the gingerroot, parsley, sesame oil, vinegar, and sugar. Stir with a fork until blended.
4. Add the onion, sweet peppers, and chili peppers to the skillet. Cook for 3 minutes. The peppers will be tender but not soft.
5. Return the pork to the skillet along with the contents of the bowl. Bring the mixture to a boil. Let it boil for 1 minute, then reduce the heat and simmer for 2 minutes. The onions should still be crisp.

6 SERVINGS

111

Jalapeño Pepper Dip

Mix this up several hours ahead of time so that the flavors will have time to seep into every crevice. Serve it in a dip dish and surround it with corn chips, tortilla chips, or slices of zucchini and top with a sprig of parsley. It will *look* bland and harmless. It isn't.

1 container (8-ounce) cottage cheese
3 garlic cloves, peeled and sliced in half
1–2 fresh jalapeño peppers, seeded
2 scallions, white part only
1 tablespoon fresh parsley, leaves only

1. Scoop the cottage cheese into a blender or food processor and give it a whirl.
2. Add the garlic, jalapeños, scallions, and parsley and process until very smooth.
3. Pour into a serving dish and chill for 3 to 5 hours.

25 SERVINGS
ON CHIPS

112

Scallion Omelette with Marjoram

The oils remain in dried herbs, so they are more concentrated than fresh ones. If you can't find fresh marjoram for this omelette, use dried and cut the amount in half. Marjoram is a cousin to oregano but has a more delicate taste.

2 tablespoons extra virgin olive oil
½ cup chopped scallions, green and white parts
2 ripe tomatoes, chopped
1 cup crumbled feta cheese

2 teaspoons minced fresh marjoram
8 eggs
½ cup water
Salt and freshly ground pepper
3 tablespoons butter

1. In a medium-size skillet, heat the oil and sauté the scallions and tomatoes for about 3 minutes or until they are soft.
2. Remove from heat and stir in the feta cheese and marjoram. Set aside.
3. Beat the eggs until they are pale yellow. With a fork, blend in the water and salt and pepper to taste.
4. In a large skillet, melt the butter and, when it is foamy, pour in the egg mixture. Cook over medium heat until set, lifting the edges with a spatula to let the uncooked eggs run underneath. Spread the tomato and scallion mixture over the middle of the omelette and fold one half over the other.
5. Serve immediately on a preheated platter.

4 SERVINGS

Shallots and Tarragon Omelette

If there's a person in your house who can't eat eggs because of cholesterol concerns, do what the restaurants do: Use egg substitute. Though yellow in color, they're actually only the whites. Cook them with shallots and herbs, and the egg lover will no longer be deprived.

Vegetable spray
1 shallot, finely chopped
1 carton egg substitute
1 teaspoon minced fresh tarragon

1. Coat a medium-size skillet with the vegetable spray, heat, and add the chopped shallot. Cook slowly for about 10 minutes, less if you want the shallots to be crunchy.
2. Pour in the egg substitute and cook on low heat, lifting the edges to let the uncooked eggs run underneath. At the last minute, sprinkle the tarragon over the top and fold it in half like an omelette. Serve immediately.

2 SERVINGS

Turnovers and Thyme

Freshly baked turnovers enclosing a tasty filling are appealing little pockets. Choose a favorite mushroom and, for variety, substitute chervil or savory for the thyme.

¼ cup low-fat cream cheese, at room temperature
2 sticks butter
1½ cups plus 2 tablespoons sifted unbleached all-purpose white flour
2 medium yellow onions, minced
½ pound fresh mushroom caps and stems, minced
½ teaspoon salt
1 teaspoon minced fresh thyme
2 teaspoons minced fresh parsley
1 garlic clove, minced
¼ cup yogurt
1 egg, beaten

1. In a food processor, combine the cream cheese, all but 3 tablespoons of the butter, and all but 2 tablespoons of the flour until a soft dough forms. Wrap in wax paper and refrigerate at least 1 hour.
2. Preheat the oven to 450°F.

3. In a saucepan, melt the remaining 3 tablespoons of butter and sauté the onions for 2 minutes. Add the mushrooms and cook until both are tender.
4. Stir in the salt, thyme, parsley, garlic, and the remaining 2 tablespoons of flour. Turn off the heat. Add the yogurt, stirring to combine.
5. On a lightly floured board, roll out half the dough to a ¼-inch thickness. Cut into 4-inch squares and place a teaspoon of the mushroom mixture on each. Brush the edges with egg and fold the dough over, forming triangles.
6. Press the edges closed with the tines of a fork, making a border. Prick the tops with two or three small holes and place them on an ungreased cookie sheet. Brush the tops with egg.
7. Continue this process with the rest of the dough, baking each batch as it is completed. Bake for 12 to 15 minutes or until golden.

ABOUT 4 DOZEN

Cheesy Bread with Thyme

Here's a classy way to change an old-fashioned baking-powder biscuit into a cheesy bread flavored with poppy seeds and thyme. Poppy seeds are a commodity that can be traced all the way back to the Sumerians, who described their medicinal uses of the plant on clay tablets.

1 *stick butter*
1 *large yellow onion, chopped (½ cup)*
1 *egg, lightly beaten*
½ *cup buttermilk*
1½ *cups unbleached all-purpose flour*
2 *teaspoons baking powder*
4 *ounces sharp cheddar cheese, shredded (1 cup)*
3 *tablespoons minced fresh thyme*
1 *tablespoon poppy seeds*

1. Preheat the oven to 350°F and grease an 8-inch square pan.
2. In a small skillet, melt 1 tablespoon of the butter and sauté the onion until it is soft and golden.
3. Combine the egg and buttermilk in a large bowl.
4. In a separate bowl, sift together the flour and baking powder and cut in 5 tablespoons of the butter. Blend into the egg and buttermilk mixture.

5. Add the onion and ½ cup of the cheese.
6. Melt the remaining 2 tablespoons of butter and combine with the rest of the cheese, the thyme, and the poppy seeds. Spread the dough in the pan and pour the cheese mixture over the top.
7. Bake 20 to 25 minutes, cut into squares, and serve hot.

16 SQUARES

In the language of herbs and flowers,
thyme represents courage.

Dill Cornbread with Sausage

Hot sausage adds a little spice to this cornbread, which would be an unusual item on a brunch buffet or even a main dish at supper. Of course, the sausage could be sweet instead; in fact, the bread can be made without any sausage at all. If you like dill, try doubling it.

2 tablespoons butter
3 medium onions, thinly sliced
½ pound hot Italian sausage
2 cups unbleached all-purpose
    flour
1 cup yellow cornmeal
¼ cup sugar

½ teaspoon baking soda
2 eggs
¼ cup vegetable oil
1¾ cup plain low-fat yogurt
¼ cup snipped dill
Salt and freshly ground pepper

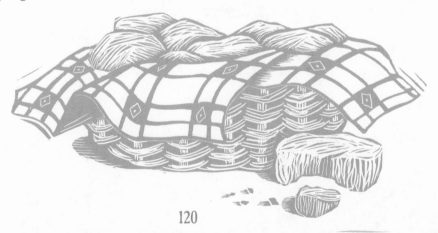

1. Preheat the oven to 400°F and grease a 10-inch round baking dish, at least 1½ inches deep.
2. Melt the butter in a medium-size skillet and sauté the onions until they are soft and golden.
3. Remove the casings from the sausage. Slice the sausage about ¼ inch thick and bake in a shallow pan for 15 minutes. Drain off the fat, turn the oven down to 350°F, and spread the sausage in the baking dish.
4. Combine the flour, cornmeal, sugar, and baking soda in a large bowl.
5. In a small bowl, beat 1 egg and combine with the oil, 1 cup of the yogurt, and the dill. Blend into the dry ingredients until everything is just mixed. Pour over the sausage slices.
6. Spread the onions on top of the batter. Combine the rest of the yogurt, the other egg, and a dash of salt and pepper and pour over the onion layer.
7. Bake for 25 to 30 minutes or until a toothpick inserted near the center comes out clean.

20 PIECES

Chinese Green-Onion Pancakes

A crepe, a tortilla, a pancake — every country seems to have its blintz, a delicate little flour product that can be enhanced with all sorts of fillings and can appear as the prologue, the main drama, or the curtain call. These traditional Chinese pancakes are made with the simplest of ingredients, and they are a treasure on the table, either as a first course or, if you make enough, as a lunch entrée with salad. Cake flour ensures tenderness, so it's worth the effort to get it.

2 cups cake flour
1 teaspoon salt
1 cup plus 2 tablespoons
   peanut oil
1 cup boiling water

4 tablespoons unbleached
   all-purpose flour
1 bunch scallions (6 or 7)
¼ cup sesame oil
2 tablespoons minced fresh parsley

1. Combine the flour and salt, stir in 2 tablespoons of the peanut oil, and add the boiling water, mixing until a ball of dough starts to form.
2. If the dough is sticky, work in as much of the all-purpose flour as is necessary to make it smooth. Knead for 4 or 5 minutes, adding flour as needed to get a smooth, elastic dough. Cover with plastic wrap. Set aside for 20 minutes.
3. In the meantime, clean and mince the green and white parts of the scallions, removing the roots and at least 1 inch from the tops. You should have ½ cup.

4. On a lightly floured surface, make a long, ropelike roll out of the dough, about 1 inch in diameter. Divide it into 16 parts.
5. Keeping the other pieces covered with plastic wrap, take one piece of the roll and, using a rolling pin, form a 5-inch circle. Brush with sesame oil, sprinkle with some of the scallions and a pinch of parsley, and roll it up, pinching the ends to seal.
6. Coil the roll into a circle, pinch the end to secure it, and set it aside on a floured platter. Repeat this process with the other 15 pieces and let them stand for about 30 minutes.
7. Roll out the coils again, this time into 4-inch circles, and leave for another 30 minutes. The pancakes can be stacked with wax paper between them.
8. Preheat the oven to warm. Heat a heavy skillet and, when it is hot, add the remaining cup of peanut oil. Fry the pancakes until they are golden brown and a little crispy on both sides. Remove with a slotted spatula and place on paper towels to drain some of the oil.
9. As they are cooked, the pancakes can be transferred to a cookie sheet in the warm oven.

16 PANCAKES

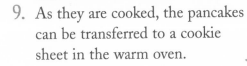

Onion Chowder with Sage

Say "chowder" and you think of clam, corn, or fish chowder. Each usually has onions as an ingredient. So why not go for the onions and forget the rest?

3 tablespoons butter
2 cups chopped yellow onions
1 garlic clove, minced
2 tablespoons minced fresh sage
1¼ pounds potatoes, peeled and
    diced (4 cups)

1½ quarts boiling water
1 teaspoon salt
Freshly ground pepper
1 quart milk, warmed
2 teaspoons minced fresh thyme
2 tablespoons chopped fresh parsley

1. In a large soup pot, melt the butter and cook the onions slowly until they are golden. For the last 5 minutes, add the garlic and sage. (If you want to make this soup without fat, substitute chicken broth for the butter.)
2. Add the potatoes and the boiling water. Reduce heat and simmer for 25 minutes or until the potatoes are tender. Add the salt, pepper to taste, milk, and thyme.
3. Reheat but do not boil. Serve the chowder in preheated bowls and garnish with the parsley.

3½ QUARTS

Highly esteemed as a healing herb, sage derives its name from the Latin salvia, *"to heal."*

Vichyssoise with Parsley

In the winter, call it leek and potato soup and serve it with chunks of the vegetables, hot as can be to dispel the cold of January or February. In summer, purée it smooth as silk, chill it, and present it in frosty glass soup plates, with a sprig of parsley and a chip of red pepper on top, to battle the heat of an August day.

2 *tablespoons butter*
2 *cups leeks, sliced into 1-inch pieces*
2 *tablespoons minced fresh Italian flat-leaf parsley*
    plus 6 whole sprigs
1½ *pounds potatoes, peeled and diced (5 cups)*
4 *cups chicken broth*
1 *cup light cream or low-fat milk*
⅛ *teaspoon white pepper*
  Salt
½ *sweet red pepper, cut in six pieces*

1. Melt the butter in a large soup pot and sauté the leeks about 4 minutes or until they are as limp as a well-cooked noodle. After the first minute or so, add the minced parsley.

2. Add the potatoes and the chicken broth. Bring to a boil, then reduce the heat to low and simmer for 15 to 20 minutes or until the potatoes are tender.

3. If you want to serve the soup hot, stir in the cream or milk, the pepper, and salt to taste. Reheat without bringing to a boil.
4. If you want a formal or chilled soup, let it cool a little and then purée in a blender. Stir in the cream or milk and the pepper. Season to taste with the salt. Chill well and garnish with parsley sprigs and a piece of red pepper.

6 SERVINGS

French Onion Soup

The French make any number of onion soups, but on American menus the name has come to mean a certain hearty blend of onions, beef broth, and flavorings, topped with a crust of bread and some kind of cheese. Here's one way to do it, using thyme.

4 tablespoons butter
5 cups of yellow onions, peeled and thinly sliced
2 garlic cloves, chopped
3 teaspoons minced fresh thyme
8 cups beef broth
Salt and freshly ground pepper
Olive oil
6 slices of French bread (baguette)
8 ounces Gruyère cheese, shredded (2 cups)

1. Melt the butter in a soup pot and add the onions. Cook the onions over low heat for 15 to 20 minutes, turning them frequently. They should be golden but not browned. Add the garlic and thyme and cook another 3 minutes.
2. Add the beef broth, bring to a boil, then reduce to a simmer for 20 minutes. Taste and add salt and pepper if needed, remembering that the broth, butter, and cheese all have salt.

3. While the soup is cooking, brush oil on both sides of the French bread slices. Place in the oven at 325°F and bake for about 10 minutes.
4. Preheat the broiler. Using individual ovenproof soup bowls, place a slice of bread in each and put a teaspoonful of cheese on the bread. Fill the bowls with hot soup and cover with the rest of the cheese.
5. Place the bowls under the broiler for about five minutes or until the cheese is bubbling. Serve immediately.

6 SERVINGS

Marshoushy

Bulgur, a tasty, cracked wheat, is a staple in the Middle East and has become well known to health-food devotees and tabbouleh lovers in the United States. This Lebanese salad, brought home by my traveling sister, takes a slightly different tack. Like tabbouleh, however, it's minty.

½ cup bulgur
½ cup boiling water
½ cup olive oil
6 yellow onions, chopped (2 cups)
½ jalapeño pepper, seeded and finely chopped
1 medium cabbage, finely chopped
1 can (8 ounces) tomato sauce
2 tablespoons finely chopped mint
Salt
Spinach or lettuce leaves
Sprigs of fresh mint for garnish

1. In a small bowl, soak the bulgur in the boiling water. Set aside for about 20 minutes until softened and then drain if any liquid remains.
2. Heat the oil in a medium skillet and sauté the onions until they are light brown. Stir in the chopped jalapeño.

3. Add the cabbage and cook over low heat for 5 to 10 minutes, stirring occasionally. The cabbage should be a little crisp rather than soft.
4. Stir in the bulgur. Add the tomato sauce, mint, and salt to taste. Simmer 20 minutes, stirring occasionally.
5. Refrigerate for about 2 hours. Serve in a mound on spinach or lettuce leaves, garnished with sprigs of mint.

6 SERVINGS

131

Green Onions and Oregano
with Garbanzo Beans

Garbanzo beans, also known as chickpeas, come dried or canned. If you decide to use dried beans, cover them in water, soak overnight, drain, and then cook them for an hour or until tender. Otherwise, use the canned beans, which are also excellent — especially with fresh oregano and parsley.

3 cups garbanzo beans, cooked
Juice of 2 lemons
4 tablespoons olive oil
Salt and freshly ground pepper
4 green onions, sliced in thin rings
2 teaspoons minced fresh oregano
2 tablespoons chopped fresh parsley
Frilly lettuce leaves

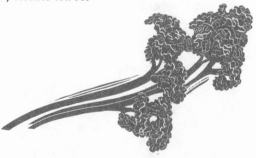

1. Heat the garbanzo beans to a boil, drain, and place in a salad bowl.
2. Combine the lemon juice, oil, salt and pepper to taste, onions, and oregano in a jar with a tightly fitting lid, then shake well. Pour over the warm beans and toss gently to avoid crushing the beans.
3. Sprinkle the parsley over the top, cover with plastic wrap, and chill. Serve on a bed of frilly lettuce.

SERVES 4

Oregano is said to calm upset stomachs, headaches, and other complaints of the nerves.

Dilled Scallion Salad

For part of the summer, you can get scallions or green onions by thinning the onions in the garden. But by the time the cucumbers come along, the onions are too big for that. So you need to plant Japanese bunching onions, which grow lovely stalks but not large bulbs.

6 scallions
2 medium young cucumbers
¼ cup snipped dill
4 tablespoons white wine vinegar
1 tablespoon sugar
Freshly ground black pepper

1. Remove the roots and the top ½ inch or so of the scallions, then slice them lengthwise into quarters. Cut the shredded lengths into 1-inch pieces.
2. Peel and slice the cucumbers paper thin.
3. Place a layer of cucumbers in a shallow bowl, top with a layer of onions, and sprinkle with dill. Continue layering until the vegetables are all used.
4. Combine the vinegar and sugar, stirring or shaking until the sugar is dissolved. Pour the dressing over the vegetables, cover with plastic wrap, and chill for about 1 hour.

4 SERVINGS

*During the Middle Ages, drinking wine with a bit of dill
was believed to enhance passion.*

South-of-the-Border Salad

On a hot summer day, a glass bowl full of well-chilled vegetables and herbs, including tender scallions from the garden, will be the perfect accompaniment for grilled chicken or fish. If cilantro is not your favorite herb, substitute parsley.

2 cucumbers, shredded (4 cups)
3 well-ripened tomatoes, chopped (2 cups)
¾ cup minced scallions, white and green parts
¼ cup minced sweet green pepper
¼ cup minced sweet red pepper
Juice of 2 limes (⅓ cup)
¼ cup extra virgin olive oil
2 tablespoons minced fresh cilantro
Salt and freshly ground black pepper
½ jalapeño pepper, seeded and minced

1. Place the cucumbers, tomatoes, scallions, and peppers in a large glass bowl. Whisk the lime juice and oil together with the cilantro, salt and pepper to taste, and jalapeño.
2. Pour the dressing over the vegetables and toss gently until all are coated. Chill.

6 TO 8 SERVINGS

Cilantro seeds — or coriander — were found in the tombs of pharaohs.

Pissaladière Niçoise

If it's *Niçoise*, it has olives, garlic, olive oil, tomatoes, basil, anchovies — some or all. They are ingredients that relish living together: Their aroma tantalizes the nostrils during cooking, their colors please the eye, their taste fulfills expectations. Pizza is not the most elegant way to sample *Niçoise*, but it's a good one.

1 package dry yeast	2 garlic cloves, chopped
1¼ cups lukewarm water	15 black olives or Greek olives, pitted
3 cups unbleached all-purpose flour	1 large ripe tomato
1 teaspoon salt	6 anchovies
1 tablespoon sugar	1 tablespoon minced fresh basil
6 tablespoons olive oil	½ cup grated and mixed Parmesan
6 large Spanish onions, sliced (about 4 cups)	and Romano cheeses

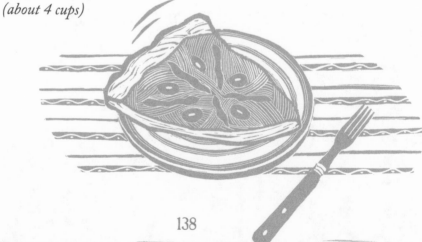

138

1. Dissolve the yeast in ¼ cup of the lukewarm water and let stand for 3 or 4 minutes.
2. Sift 2½ cups of the flour, the salt, and the sugar into a bowl. Stir in the rest of the water and add the yeast mixture.
3. Add 2 tablespoons of the olive oil and knead for 2 or 3 minutes. Add more flour to make the dough easy to handle. Knead until smooth.
4. Place the dough in an oiled bowl, cover with a towel, and let rise for about 45 minutes.
5. While the dough is rising, heat the remaining 4 tablespoons of olive oil in a large skillet, add the onions, and cook over low heat slowly for 30 to 40 minutes. They should be soft and translucent, not brown, so temperature is crucial. Add the garlic for the last 10 minutes. Remove from heat and let cool.
6. Preheat the oven to 400°F. Chop the olives. Cut the tomato crosswise and scoop out most of the seeds, then chop it.
7. Roll out or form the dough into a 12-inch circle in a slightly oiled pizza pan. Layer on the cooked onions, arrange the olives and anchovies in a star pattern on top of the onions, and scatter the chopped tomato and the basil over the top. Sprinkle with the grated cheeses.
8. Bake for about 15 minutes or until the edges of the dough have browned slightly and the cheese has melted.

6–8 PIECES

Pasta with Garlic and Herb Sauce

Red sauce is what most people eat on pasta. But pasta takes to so many kinds of sauces that it's a good idea to branch out now and then. This sauce, chock-full of herbs, makes a great vegetarian main dish and can be served over linguini, fusilli, or one of the short, curly noodles, like rotini, that hold a sauce so well.

> 1 stick butter
> ¼ cup chopped garlic (about 24 medium cloves)
> 2 tablespoons finely chopped fresh basil
> ½ teaspoon finely chopped fresh rosemary
> ½ teaspoon finely chopped fresh thyme
>   White pepper
> 2 cups half-and-half or light cream
> 1½ pounds pasta
>   Salt
> ¼ cup minced fresh Italian flat-leaf parsley

1. Start a large pot of water boiling for the pasta. In the meantime, melt the butter in a large skillet and gently sauté the garlic for 2 minutes. Add the basil, rosemary, thyme, pepper to taste, and half-and-half or cream.

2. Simmer slowly for approximately 5 minutes, until the cream is reduced and the sauce has thickened. Drop the pasta into the boiling water and cook according to package directions.
3. Salt the sauce to taste and stir in the parsley.
4. Drain the pasta, place in a warmed pasta bowl, pour the sauce over the top, and mix lightly.

6 SERVINGS

Potatoes, Onions, and Oregano

You can fry them together, bake them together, or simmer them together in a soup. Potatoes and onions are friends. In this case, combined with fresh oregano and a few other ingredients, they become a meal. Try this dish with a salad of varied greens and vinaigrette dressing. If green tomatoes aren't available, try substituting one large red or yellow pepper.

¼ *pound turkey sausage, spicy or plain*
2 *medium onions, peeled and chopped*
1 *cup unbleached all-purpose flour*
1 *pound of sharp cheddar cheese, shredded*
2 *teaspoons minced fresh oregano*
8 *medium potatoes, peeled and thinly sliced*
3 *large green tomatoes, thinly sliced*
Salt and freshly ground black pepper
½ *cup low-fat milk*

1. Preheat the broiler and brown the turkey sausage on a rack so any grease will drain off. Remove, slice thin, and set aside.
2. Preheat the oven to 350°F and grease a 9 x 13-inch baking dish. In a bowl, combine the onions, flour, cheese, oregano, and salt and pepper to taste.
3. Alternating layers, fill the pan with the potatoes, tomatoes, and turkey sausage. Between each layer, thinly sprinkle the onion and cheese mixture and add salt and pepper to taste. Continue layering until all the ingredients are used, ending with a layer of cheese. Pour the milk over the top.
4. Bake for 1 hour or until the potatoes are soft and the cheese is bubbly.

6 SERVINGS

The name oregano is derived from the Greek origanum,
which means "joy of the mountains."

Thyme and Onion Pie

The Chinese have a gift for taking a small amount of meat — chicken, pork, or beef — and surrounding it with vegetables and rice or noodles in such a way that you have the illusion of considerably more. This onion pie, inexpensive and fragrant with thyme, does much the same thing. It can be made with a prepared pie shell, a flaky pastry of your own, or this baking-powder biscuit crust.

CRUST INGREDIENTS
- 1 cup flour
- 1½ teaspoons baking powder
- ½ teaspoon salt
- 2 tablespoons butter
- ½ cup low-fat milk

FILLING INGREDIENTS
- 3 tablespoons butter
- 4 large yellow onions, chopped (2 cups)
- 1 tablespoon minced fresh thyme
- 3 eggs
- ¼ teaspoon ground cloves
- ½ teaspoon salt
- Freshly ground black pepper
- 1 cup low-fat yogurt
- 3 slices Canadian bacon or thinly sliced ham

1. Preheat the oven to 350°F. Sift the flour and combine with baking powder, salt, butter, and milk for the baking-powder biscuit crust. Roll out the dough to a ¼-inch thickness and line the bottom of a 9-inch pie pan, leaving extra around the edge.
2. Double the extra dough over and crimp into a fluted rim around the pan. Bake the crust for 5 minutes, remove from the oven, and increase the oven temperature to 400°F.
3. While the crust is baking, make the filling. Melt the butter in a large skillet, then sauté the onions with the minced thyme until the onions are soft but not browned. Remove from heat.
4. In a small bowl, whisk the eggs. Add the eggs, cloves, salt, and pepper to taste to the onions and toss gently. Then add the yogurt. Pour the mixture into the pie pan.
5. Cut the Canadian bacon or ham into small squares and arrange decoratively over the top of the onion mixture. Bake about 15 minutes or until the meat is crisp and the crust is light brown. Cut into wedges and serve immediately.

4–6 SERVINGS

Savory Quiche with Onions

Perhaps real men don't eat quiche, or perhaps they've never tried it. In any case, they should like this one. It's not the least bit wimpy, what with a high onion content and the bite of cayenne.

PASTRY DOUGH FOR QUICHE

1⅓ cups unbleached all-purpose flour
½ cup very cold butter, cut into inch-long pieces
¼ cup ice water
Olive oil

QUICHE INGREDIENTS

3 tablespoons extra virgin olive oil
2 tablespoons butter
1½ pounds white onions, peeled and sliced
1 cup half-and-half
½ teaspoon cayenne pepper
2 teaspoons minced fresh savory
Salt
4 eggs
¼ cup minced fresh parsley

1. To make the pastry dough, place the flour and butter in a food processor and process for no more than 10 seconds. The mixture will have the consistency of meal. Slowly pour the ice water through the feed tube while the processor is running. Stop when the dough forms a ball. Remove and shape into a flat round.
2. On a lightly floured board, roll out the pastry until it is large enough for a 10-inch quiche or pie pan. Brush a thin layer of the oil on the pan and roll out the pastry slightly larger than the pan. Crimp the edges.
3. Preheat the oven to 350°F. Heat the oil and the butter in a large skillet, add the onions, and cook over low heat for at least 30 minutes. The onions will be soft and nearly translucent — but not browned.
4. In a bowl, combine the half-and-half with the cayenne, savory, and salt to taste. Add the eggs and beat until foamy. Stir in the parsley.
5. Spread the onions over the pastry in an even layer. Pour in the egg mixture, making sure it trickles down through the layer of onion. Bake for 30 to 35 minutes or until firm and browned on top.
6. Cut in wedges and serve warm.

8–10 SERVINGS

Deviled Shrimp and Onion Salad

Rich, roasted peppers, black olives, yellow lemon, and red onion put a riot of color around pink shrimp in this summer salad. Serve it in a cut glass or black bowl for a spectacular effect.

2 pounds fresh shrimp
1 lemon, thinly sliced
1 red onion, thinly sliced
½ cup chopped black Greek olives
2 tablespoons chopped roasted
    sweet green peppers
1 bay leaf
Juice of 1 large lemon
    (about ½ cup)

¼ cup extra virgin olive oil
1 tablespoon white wine vinegar
2 garlic cloves, put through a press
1 tablespoon dry mustard
¼ teaspoon cayenne
Salt and freshly ground pepper
½ cup coarsely chopped fresh parsley

1. Shell and devein the shrimp. Cook for 3 minutes in lightly salted boiling water.
2. Drain the shrimp and place in a large salad bowl to cool. Add the lemon, onion, olives, and roasted peppers. Toss.
3. Crush the bay leaf very fine with a mortar and pestle or in a blender. Combine in a small bowl with the lemon juice, olive oil, vinegar, garlic, dry mustard, and cayenne. Mix thoroughly and add salt and pepper to taste.

4. Pour the dressing over the shrimp and toss gently, taking care not to break the shrimp.
5. Sprinkle the parsley over the top, cover tightly with plastic wrap, and refrigerate for at least 2 hours.

4 SERVINGS

Sole with Chives and Leeks

Here's a dish that embraces three members of the allium family: leeks, chives, and shallots. Beat and heat gently to make sure the sauce doesn't curdle; add fresh chopped parsley at the last minute for a bright contrast with the pale green of the leeks and the white fish.

6 tablespoons butter
6 medium leeks, sliced
¼ cup snipped fresh chives
2 shallots, peeled and chopped (2 tablespoons)
¼ cup dry white wine
¾ cup half-and-half
4 egg yolks
¼ teaspoon white pepper
2 teaspoons lemon juice
Salt
6 sole or flounder fillets
¼ cup chopped fresh parsley

1. Preheat the oven to 325°F.
2. Melt 2 tablespoons of the butter in a heavy skillet and sauté the leeks 3 to 5 minutes or until they are limp. Transfer to a bowl and set aside.
3. Melt the rest of the butter and sauté the chives and shallots for 2 minutes. Add the wine and half-and-half and simmer for about 1 minute.
4. In a small bowl, beat the egg yolks and add about a tablespoon of the sauce to them. Add the yolks to the rest of the sauce.
5. Heat gently. Add the white pepper, lemon juice, and salt to taste, then heat until the sauce thickens slightly. Mix about a quarter of the sauce with the leeks.
6. Spoon the leek mixture onto each sole fillet, then roll up the fillets. Place the rolls seam-side down in a baking dish, pour the remaining sauce over the fish, and cover with aluminum foil.
7. Bake for 30 minutes, uncover, sprinkle the parsley over the top, and serve.

6 SERVINGS

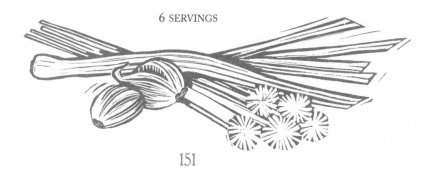

Chive and Dill Sauce for Fish

One of the great things about chives is that you can plant a little bunch almost anywhere among your perennials and they'll be there, ready to use. If you live in the snowy north, their green shoots are a reassuring sign of spring. A member of the onion family, chives work well both for mild onion flavor and as a garnish. Use the feathery leaves of dill in this sauce and garnish each plate with a handsome head of dill in bloom.

4 tablespoons sweet butter
2 tablespoons snipped fresh chives
1 teaspoon lemon juice
½ teaspoon dry mustard
2 teaspoons finely snipped fresh dill
4 fish fillets

1. Melt the butter in a medium-size skillet, add the chives, and cook for about 2 minutes over low heat.
2. Blend in the lemon juice, dry mustard, and dill.
3. Bake, broil, or poach the fish fillets. Pour the sauce over the fillets and serve.

4 SERVINGS

Onions, Mushrooms, and Tarragon

As a sauce for sole or a relish on the side, this combination of onions, hot peppers, shiitakes, and tarragon adds zip.

2	*large white onions, thinly sliced*
2	*teaspoons salt*
1½	*tablespoons extra virgin olive oil*
6	*large shiitake caps, sliced*
1	*habanero or other hot chile pepper, finely chopped*
1	*tablespoon chopped fresh parsley*
½	*cup white wine vinegar*
2	*tablespoons chopped fresh tarragon*
1	*cup plain lowfat yogurt*

1. Place the onions in a glass bowl, sprinkle with the salt, cover with cold water, and let stand for 15 to 20 minutes.
2. Heat the oil in a skillet and sauté the shiitake slices over low heat for 5 minutes. Add the pepper and parsley. Cook another 5 minutes. Set aside.
3. Drain the onions. Combine the vinegar and tarragon and pour over the onions. Let the mixture stand for about 5 minutes.
4. Combine the onions with the mushrooms, pepper, and herb mixture. Stir in the yogurt. Serve chilled or at room temperature.

2 CUPS

Elissa's Jambalaya

Once upon a time, there was a recipe. Then Tim got his hands on it and tinkered with it. He passed it on to Ann, who changed it some more. She gave it to Elissa, who decided on the turkey sausage. When it came to us, we jiggled it a little, too. Try it, then change it again if you like.

2–3 tablespoons extra virgin olive oil
5 large onions, chopped
2 sweet green peppers, chopped
4 ribs of celery, chopped
4 garlic cloves, chopped
1 can (28 ounces) crushed tomatoes
2 cans (16 ounces) chicken broth
1 package (6 to 8) turkey sausages
½ cup diced ham
¼ cup minced fresh parsley
2 tablespoons hot sauce
¼ cup soy sauce
3 tablespoons minced fresh thyme
Freshly ground black pepper
1½ pounds shrimp, shelled and deveined
1½ pounds bay scallops
2 cups cooked rice

1. Heat the oil in a Dutch oven or soup pot. Add the onions and sauté for 2 or 3 minutes. Add the green peppers, celery, and garlic. Continue to cook until the vegetables begin to soften.
2. Add the crushed tomatoes and the chicken broth. Cover and simmer for 30 minutes.

3. In the meantime, place the turkey sausages in a shallow pan and bake in the oven for 15 minutes or until they are browned. When they are cool enough to handle, cut them into ¾-inch slices.
4. Add the ham, parsley, hot sauce, soy sauce, thyme, and black pepper to taste to the onion-tomato mixture. Cover and simmer another 20 minutes.
5. Add the sausage, shrimp, scallops, and rice to the pot. Cover and simmer a final 25 minutes.

SERVES 10–12

Onion Rice with Tarragon

It's a little hard to tell whether this is an onion dish with rice or a rice dish with onions — but it's easy to tell that it's delicious. There are, however, a lot of onions to peel, so the cook may be sobbing before all is done.

2 tablespoons unsalted butter
6 large onions, sliced
2 teaspoons minced fresh tarragon
4 quarts of water with ½ teaspoon salt
2 cups uncooked brown rice
Salt and freshly ground pepper
½ cup white wine or water
¼ cup half-and-half
4 ounces Gruyère cheese, grated (1 cup)

1. Preheat the oven to 300°F.
2. Melt the butter in a large ovenproof skillet or casserole dish. Add the onions and tarragon and cook over low heat until they are buttery and soft.
3. In a large saucepan, bring the salted water to a boil, add the rice, and boil for 5–10 minutes to soften. Drain the rice and add it to the onions, along with salt and pepper to taste. Cover and bake for 50 to 60 minutes. (The onions will provide enough liquid for the rice to cook.)

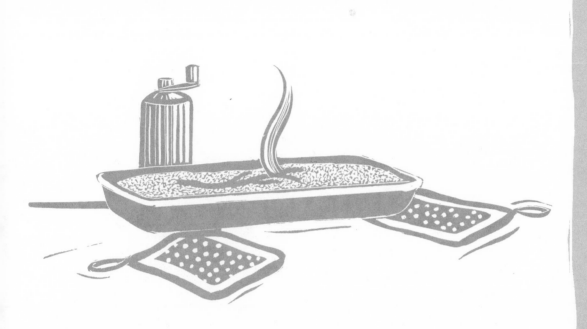

4. When done, cool the casserole slightly, then refrigerate. Up to this point, the recipe may be prepared the day before.
5. To serve, add the white wine or water and reheat over low heat. In the meantime, mix the half-and-half with the cheese and heat gently. When the rice is hot, combine the rice and cheese mixtures.

10 SERVINGS

Walter's Herbed Chicken with Onions

It's hard to get a recipe from Walter because he's the kind of cook who surveys the refrigerator and cupboards, gets out a pot, and starts putting various things in it. (His friends can testify that the method works for him just about every time.) He has tried here to provide real quantities for ingredients and says this should cook until it's like stew, with the onions turning to juice and becoming almost unrecognizable.

6 *medium yellow onions*	6 *medium-size ripe tomatoes*
3 *garlic cloves*	3 *boneless, skinless chicken*
1 *tablespoon minced fresh oregano*	*breasts, halved*
¼ *cup light soy sauce*	1 *tablespoon minced fresh basil*

1. Peel and thinly slice the onions. Crush the garlic. Place them in a 2- or 3-quart casserole with the oregano. Add the soy sauce.
2. Preheat the oven to 325°F.
3. Wash and slice the tomatoes about ½-inch thick. Arrange the chicken breasts in a single layer atop the onions and cover them with a single layer of sliced tomatoes. Sprinkle the basil over the top and cover the casserole.
4. Bake in the oven for 2 hours. (It can bake up to 3 hours if guests are late.) If the dish seems to be cooking too fast, turn the oven down to 300°F.

6 SERVINGS

Veal Scallopini with Onions

Start this with really good veal — ask the butcher to pound it thin. If it's not really thin, put the slices between pieces of wax paper and pound it some more. With its butter, oil, herbs, onions, and white wine, this is a superb dinner party dish.

1½ pounds veal scallopini,
      pounded thin
4 tablespoons flour
Salt and freshly ground black pepper
2 tablespoons extra virgin olive oil
3 tablespoons butter

2 yellow onions, peeled and sliced
2 tablespoons chopped fresh
      oregano
2 tablespoons chopped fresh parsley
½ cup dry white wine

1. Dredge the scallopini in the flour, adding salt and pepper to taste. Shake to remove excess flour. Heat the oil in a large skillet and quickly brown the veal on both sides, removing the pieces to a warm plate as they are done. Each slice will take only a minute or so per side.

2. Pour any excess oil out of the pan, but do not rinse the pan. Melt the butter and sauté the onions until they are tender. Add the oregano and parsley and return the veal to the pan, turning the slices to coat them with onions and butter. Add the wine and simmer until everything is hot.

4 SERVINGS

159

Beef, Beer, and Bay Leaves

On a cold winter weekend, get this stew going in the morning and let it simmer its way to full flavor. Once it's made, you can refrigerate it, skim off any fat that appears on the surface, and reheat it for dinner.

¼ cup unbleached all-purpose flour
¼ teaspoon salt
¼ teaspoon freshly ground black pepper
2 pounds lean beef, trimmed of fat and cut into cubes
12 small onions, peeled
1 bottle (12-ounces) dark beer
2 cups beef broth
2 cups water
2 tablespoons red wine vinegar
1 tablespoon brown sugar
2 garlic cloves, chopped
2 tablespoons chopped fresh marjoram
2 bay leaves

1. In a plastic bag, mix the flour, salt, and pepper. Add the beef cubes and toss until they are coated with the mixture. Shake off the excess flour.

2. In a Dutch oven or soup pot, combine the beef cubes, half the onions, the beer, the beef broth, and the water. Bring to a boil and skim off any foam that appears. Add the vinegar, brown sugar, garlic, marjoram, and bay leaves.

3. Bring to a boil again, reduce the heat, and simmer for about 1½ hours. Add the rest of the onions. Simmer for another 30 to 45 minutes or until the beef is really tender. Remove the bay leaves if they are still whole.

SERVES 4

*Bay is symbolic
of peace and victory.*

Sherried Onions with Dill

This version of creamed onions carries a hint of sherry and a touch of fresh dill.

MAIN INGREDIENTS

2 pounds small white onions
1 tablespoon finely snipped dill
¼ cup medium-dry sherry

WHITE SAUCE INGREDIENTS

4 tablespoons butter
4 tablespoons unbleached all-purpose flour
2 cups low-fat milk at room temperature

1. Peel the onions and boil them until they're just cooked but not falling apart. Drain them and place in a baking dish.
2. Preheat the oven to 325°F.
3. To prepare white sauce in microwave, cook the butter and flour for 2 minutes, stirring after the first minute. Add the milk and cook 4 minutes more, stirring after 2 minutes. If the sauce has not thickened, cook for another 2 minutes.
4. Blend the dill and the sherry into the white sauce and pour over the onions. Bake for 15 or 20 minutes.

6 SERVINGS

Savory Onions with a Glaze

With this unique dish, once you've peeled all the onions, the work is done. The other ingredients are simple to prepare, then the oven takes over. The result is an almost caramelized sweetness with a hint of cayenne.

36 *small white onions*
⅔ *stick butter*
1 *beef bouillon cube*
1 *tablespoon brown sugar*
½ *teaspoon salt*
⅛ *teaspoon cayenne*
Dash of nutmeg
Dash of ground ginger
2 *teaspoons minced fresh savory*

1. Fill a large pot with water and bring to a boil. Drop in the onions and let cook for a minute. Drain and peel the onions. Preheat oven to 350°F.
2. Melt the butter in a casserole dish in the oven. Remove and stir in the bouillon cube, brown sugar, salt, cayenne, nutmeg, ginger, and savory.
3. Add the onions and toss gently until they are well coated. Cover and bake for about 1 hour, occasionally checking to make sure the onions are not sticking to the casserole dish

6–8 SERVINGS

New-Fashioned Boiled Onions

Boiled onions, slathered with butter, salt, and pepper, were always part of our traditional Thanksgiving dinner. But they had to cook a long time, and so they'd start to separate. Delicious as the rounded layers were, you'd wish for a whole one. Here's how to keep the taste, add some new flavor, and hold the onions together using the microwave.

10 *medium yellow onions, peeled*
1 *tablespoon water*
2 *tablespoons butter*
2 *teaspoons minced fresh chervil*

1. Place the peeled, whole onions in a microwavable casserole dish with the water and butter. Cover tightly and microwave on high for 7 to 8 minutes.
2. Sprinkle the chervil over the top and serve.

4 SERVINGS

Grilled Onions with Herbs

Our friend Sel, who has tried grilling practically everything, recommends putting a piece of slate or some other fireproof slab on the grill, then placing foil packages of vegetables on the slate. You won't have to watch in dismay while nicely cooked onions slip into the fire. (Sel suggests roasting garlic, another member of the onion family, in foil on slate, too.)

8 large white or yellow onions
1 stick butter, melted
¼ cup chopped fresh parsley
1 tablespoon chopped fresh sage
1 garlic clove, minced
2 tablespoons grated Parmesan
* and Romano cheeses, mixed*

1. Peel the onions, slice about ¼ inch off the top, and hollow out the center, leaving plenty of wall. Chop what you remove.
2. In a saucepan, melt the butter and sauté the chopped onion for about a minute. Remove from heat and add the parsley, sage, garlic, and grated cheeses. Scoop the mixture into the hollowed onions.
3. Place the filled onions on heavy-duty aluminum foil and wrap them tightly. Put them on the grill for at least 30 minutes — beware of escaping steam when you open the package.

8 SERVINGS

Braised Leeks with Dill

Leeks are kind of a sleeper. You don't see them on restaurant menus very often, except in soup, and you don't eat them at home very often, either. But they're sweet, oniony, and versatile. Here they team with tomatoes, onions, and dill. (Their one disadvantage is they're hard to clean. Unless a recipe says otherwise, slit them lengthwise and flush them with water until the grit is gone.)

8 *medium leeks*
2 *tablespoons butter*
2 *tablespoons extra virgin olive oil*
2 *medium onions, peeled and sliced into rings*
2 *large ripe tomatoes, peeled and chopped*
½ *cup chicken broth*
½ *cup dry white wine*
   Salt and freshly ground black pepper
1 *tablespoon snipped fresh dill*

1. Trim the leeks, removing the coarse upper leaves and cutting off all but 2½ inches of the green leafy part. Wash thoroughly. Drain and cut each leek into 1½- to 2-inch pieces.
2. In a large skillet, melt the butter, add the oil, and sauté the onions slowly, until they are golden and translucent but not fried. Add the leeks and the tomatoes.
3. Add the chicken broth, white wine, and salt and pepper to taste. Bring to a boil, reduce the heat, and simmer gently until the leeks are tender but not mushy.
4. Transfer to a heated serving dish. Garnish with the dill and serve.

6 SERVINGS

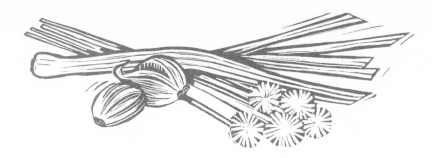

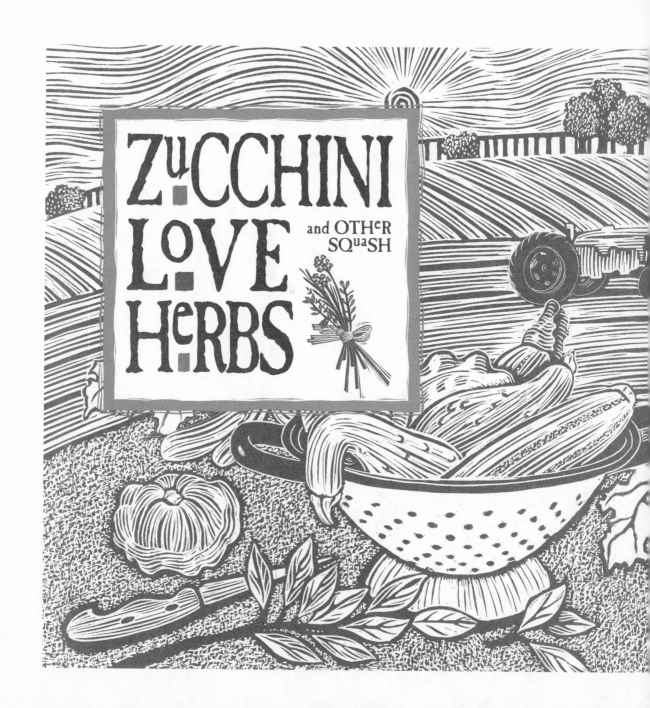

Zucchini Muffins with Lemon Thyme

Powdered buttermilk saves the cook from throwing away a forgotten half carton several days after making a dish. Keep this form of buttermilk on hand and use it often in biscuits, muffins, and pancakes.

2 cups unbleached all-purpose flour
2 teaspoons baking powder
¼ teaspoon salt
½ cup brown sugar
1 cup buttermilk, fresh or reconstituted powder
2 eggs, beaten

½ cup safflower or canola oil
1 medium zucchini, finely shredded
1 teaspoon ground cinnamon
¼ teaspoon ground ginger
¼ cup finely chopped fresh lemon thyme

1. Preheat the oven to 400°F and lightly grease a 12-cup muffin tin.
2. Sift together the flour, baking powder, salt, and sugar into a bowl.
3. In a separate bowl, combine the buttermilk, eggs, oil, and zucchini.
4. Add the dry ingredients to the buttermilk-and-egg mixture and stir well to blend.
5. Combine the cinnamon, ginger, and lemon thyme and stir into the muffin mixture. Pour into muffin cups and bake for 20 to 25 minutes.

12 MUFFINS

169

Squash Bread with Apples and Sage

Winter squash gives body, color, and moisture to a quick bread — what more could anyone want? Well, maybe some apples and cinnamon and sage.

    1¼ cups safflower oil
      1 cup brown sugar
     ¾ cup white sugar
      4 eggs or 1 carton cholesterol-free egg substitute
    1¾ cups puréed butternut squash
    1½ tablespoons minced fresh sage
      1 cup unbleached all-purpose flour
      1 cup whole-wheat flour
      2 teaspoons baking soda
      1 teaspoon ground cinnamon
     ½ teaspoon ground cloves
     ½ teaspoon ground nutmeg
     ½ teaspoon salt
      3 Northern Spy apples, peeled and chopped
     ½ cup raisins

1. Preheat the oven to 350°F. Grease and flour two 9-inch loaf pans.
2. Cream together the oil, sugars, and eggs or egg substitute. Blend in the squash purée. Add the sage.
3. Sift together the flours, baking soda, cinnamon, cloves, nutmeg, and salt. Gradually stir the flour mixture into the squash mixture, blending until smooth. Add the apples and raisins.
4. Divide the batter between the two pans and bake for 50 to 60 minutes. Cool the loaves on a rack for 10 minutes, then turn them out on the rack for complete cooling.

2 LOAVES

Squash Marmalade with Mint

Before winter is over, stored butternut or acorn squash start to soften. That's the ideal time to turn a couple of them into marmalade enhanced with fresh mint leaves.

> 2 oranges
> 2 lemons, rind and juice
> 16 cups grated winter squash
> 1 cup orange juice
> 3 inches fresh gingerroot, minced
> Pinch of salt
> 4 cups sugar
> 4 sprigs of mint, washed and patted dry

1. Sterilize four ½-pint jelly jars and two-part canning lids by boiling them for 5 minutes in water to cover.
2. Peel the oranges and lemons. Sliver the lemon rinds very thinly. In a heavy saucepan, cover the rinds with water and simmer for 5 minutes. Drain and repeat the process.
3. Cut off the tops and bottoms of the oranges and remove the pith and skin. Divide the oranges into sections, seed, and chop. Add the pieces to the drained slivers of rind.
4. Halve the lemons and squeeze out the juice.

5. Add the squash, lemon juice, orange juice, 2 tablespoons of minced gingerroot, and the salt. Bring to a boil.
6. Stir in the sugar, return the marmalade mixture to a boil, and remove it from the heat. It will be quite runny, but overcooked marmalade is rubbery. Skim off the surface foam and immediately ladle the hot marmalade into the sterilized jelly jars. Insert a sprig of mint in each jar.
7. Leave ¼ inch of head space, seal with the sterilized lids, and immerse in boiling water for 5 minutes.

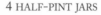

4 HALF-PINT JARS

Crispy Squash Blossoms with Savory

People keep talking about eating flowers — daylilies, marigolds, even squash blossoms. And you really can. If you experiment with squash blossoms from your own garden, pick the males (they're longer, with no tiny squash visible at the base), or you'll eliminate the main crop. Obviously, unsprayed blossoms are essential. These fried blossoms make an unusual appetizer.

FOR THE DISH
15 *squash blossoms*
⅔ *cup flour*
½ *cup water*
Peanut or canola oil for frying
Salt

1. Rinse the blossoms gently, dry well, and halve lengthwise.
2. Make a batter by gradually whisking the flour into the water.
3. Heat about ½ inch of the oil in a deep skillet or wok until it tests at 375°F. Coat a few blossoms at a time with the batter and cook, browning on both sides.
4. Drain them on paper towels and sprinkle with salt to taste. Serve immediately with mustard sauce or reheat in the oven.

30 PIECES

FOR THE SAUCE

1 tablespoon dry mustard

½ cup sugar

¼ cup honey

½ cup cider vinegar

3 tablespoons water

2 beaten eggs

2 tablespoons minced fresh savory

1. Combine the mustard, sugar, and honey in a saucepan. Stir in the vinegar and water.
2. Add the eggs and stir over medium heat until the sauce boils and thickens. Stir in the minced savory. Serve warm or refrigerate and reheat.

1½ CUPS

175

Goat Cheese, Sun-Dried Tomatoes, and Zucchini

Whatever the season, the combination of warmed goat cheese, fresh herbs, and sun-dried tomatoes will sing of summer days. This salad could be served as a special appetizer or as a side dish. You can also cut the zucchini into small wedges, attach the cheese and tomatoes with a toothpick, and serve as an hors d'oeuvre.

½ cup water
1 pound small zucchini, scrubbed
   and unpeeled
3 tablespoons extra virgin olive oil
¼ cup chopped sun-dried tomatoes
   in olive oil
Juice of 1 lemon

1 small garlic clove, minced
1 tablespoon chopped fresh chervil
2 tablespoons chopped fresh parsley
1 teaspoon capers
Salt and freshly ground black pepper
6 ounces plain chevre (goat cheese)

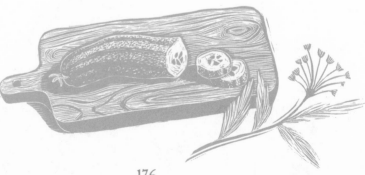

1. Bring the water to a boil in a saucepan. Slice the zucchini into ½-inch rounds and boil for 2 to 4 minutes. Remove, rinse with cold water, and drain.
2. In a small bowl, combine the oil, sun-dried tomatoes, lemon juice, garlic, chervil, parsley, capers, and salt and pepper to taste. Whisk until well blended. Place the zucchini in a bowl and cover with the dressing. Stir very gently to coat.
3. At serving time, warm the chevre for 45 seconds in a microwave oven. Arrange zucchini slices on individual serving plates and top each plate with a scoop of the warmed cheese. Serve immediately.

4 SERVINGS

A cousin of dill, chervil is one of the traditional fines herbes *so essential to French cuisine.*

Yellow Squash Cakes

These delectable little cakes spiked with fragrant herbs will be a hit at a dinner party or a summer supper in the backyard. If thyme and rosemary don't suit your palate, try chopped mint or dill or oregano — summer squash is adaptable. Just remember to take those tough stems off the thyme and really mince the spiky rosemary.

1½ teaspoons minced fresh thyme
1½ teaspoons minced fresh rosemary
2 teaspoons minced fresh parsley
1 garlic clove, minced
3 cups grated summer squash
¼ cup grated Romano cheese
½ cup grated Parmesan cheese
1 cup unbleached all-purpose flour
1 teaspoon baking powder
¼ teaspoon salt
Freshly ground black pepper
1 tablespoon extra virgin olive oil
½ tablespoon butter

1. In a medium-size bowl, combine the thyme, rosemary, parsley, and garlic. Stir in the grated squash, cheeses, flour, baking powder, salt, and pepper to taste.
2. Heat half of the oil in a large skillet and add half of the butter. Dollop tablespoons of squash batter into the skillet and cook over medium heat until golden. Flip to cook the other side. Add oil and butter as needed to prevent sticking.
3. Finished cakes may be kept warm in the oven.

25–30 CAKES

179

Zucchini Pancakes with Lemon Verbena

Put some zing into pancakes with the bite of feta cheese and the tang of lemon verbena. Serve with a dollop of yogurt or a little honey.

2 *medium zucchini, grated*
½ *teaspoon salt*
2 *eggs, beaten*
1 *tablespoon safflower or canola oil*
1 *cup crumbled feta cheese*
2 *teaspoons chopped fresh lemon verbena leaves*
¼ *cup plus 2 tablespoons unbleached all-purpose flour*
4 *tablespoons butter*

1. Place the grated zucchini in a colander, sprinkle with salt, and let stand for 30 minutes. Squeeze to remove moisture.
2. Combine the eggs, oil, feta cheese, lemon verbena, and flour in a large bowl and mix well. Stir in the zucchini.
3. Melt 1 tablespoon of the butter on a griddle and dollop tablespoons of batter to create silver-dollar-sized pancakes. Flip to brown on both sides, adding butter as needed.

1½ DOZEN PANCAKES

Summer Squash and Chervil Soup

If you want to cook with chervil, you may have to find a place for it in your garden or on your windowsill. Despite its intriguing flavor, it's not always among the fresh herbs in the market — and the dried version loses something in the transition.

> 4 *tablespoons butter*
> 2 *onions, diced*
> 2 *tablespoons chopped fresh chervil*
> 1 *tablespoon minced fresh basil*
> 1 *tablespoon minced fresh parsley*
> 6 *cups shredded yellow summer squash*
> 1 *cup sliced carrots*
> 4½ *cups chicken broth*
> ¾ *cup dry white wine*
> *Salt and freshly ground black pepper*

1. In a large soup pot, melt the butter and gently sauté the onions for 5 minutes. Stir in the chervil, basil, and parsley and cook for another 5 minutes or until the onions are soft but not browned.
2. Add the squash, carrots, broth, wine, and salt and pepper to taste. Bring to a boil, reduce the heat immediately, and simmer for 12 minutes or until the squash and carrots are tender.

6 SERVINGS

Harvest Soup with Herbs

Fall is the season for both winter squash and fresh tart apples. Bring them together, with plenty of herbs, in a soup that takes the bite out of the first frost.

> 1 *butternut or other winter squash*
> 1 *tablespoon extra virgin olive oil*
> 4 *shallots, chopped*
> 3 *tart McIntosh apples, chopped*
> 1 *teaspoon chopped fresh sage*
> 1 *teaspoon chopped fresh marjoram*
> 1 *tablespoon chopped fresh parsley*
> 3 *cups chicken broth*
> 1½ *cups fresh apple cider*
> ½ *cup dry white wine*
> *Salt and freshly ground black pepper*

1. Preheat the oven to 350°F. Scrub the squash, halve it lengthwise, and remove all seeds and stringy fibers. Lightly oil the cut surfaces and place on a baking sheet, cut side down. Bake for 35 to 45 minutes or until tender. When cool, scoop out the flesh and set aside.
2. In a soup pot, heat the oil and cook the shallots for about 5 minutes, without browning. Add the chopped apples and cook for 1 more minute.

3. Stir in the sage, marjoram, parsley, broth, cider, wine, and salt and pepper to taste. Simmer for 1 hour. Add the squash and cook for another 5 minutes.

4. In a food processor or blender, purée the mixture and return it to the soup pot. Reheat, adding more broth, cider, or wine if necessary to get the desired consistency.

6 SERVINGS

Squash Soup with Shiitakes and Thyme

The woodsiness of shiitakes cozies up nicely with fresh-smelling thyme, and the two bundle well with mellow winter squash. This recipe calls for acorn squash, but a chunk of a blue hubbard, a butternut, or even a pumpkin will do.

2 acorn squash
2 tablespoons extra virgin olive oil
2 large onions, chopped (Vidalia if they're in season)
3 garlic cloves, minced
8 medium shiitakes
1 tablespoon minced fresh thyme
2 tablespoons minced fresh parsley
¼ cup sherry or Chinese rice wine
2 cups cider
1 cup water
Zest of 1 orange
1 tablespoon light soy sauce
Salt and freshly ground black pepper
2 cups half-and-half

1. Preheat the oven to 350°F. Halve the squash lengthwise, remove the seeds and stringy fibers, and lightly oil the cut surfaces. Place them cut side down on a baking sheet and bake for 35 to 45 minutes, depending on size and variety of squash. Scoop out the flesh and measure out 4 cups.
2. Heat the oil in a soup pot and slowly cook the onions for about 10 to 12 minutes or until soft but not browned, adding the garlic after the first 5 minutes.
3. Clean the shiitakes, discard the tough stems, and chop. Add them, along with the thyme and parsley, to the onion mixture and cook for about 5 minutes.
4. Stir in the sherry or rice wine, cider, water, orange zest, and soy sauce and bring to a boil. Immediately reduce the heat to medium and mix in the mashed squash.
5. Add salt and pepper to taste, stir in the half-and-half, and bring almost to a boil. Serve immediately.

4–6 SERVINGS

The word thyme *comes from the Greek* thymon,
which means "courage."

Zucchini Provençal

The adaptable zucchini wears the mantle of Provence with aplomb. Use the garlic and basil in whatever quantity pleases your palate — neither is shy about participation.

4–5 *small zucchini (about 4 inches long)*
2 *tablespoons extra virgin olive oil*
1 *onion, thinly sliced*
1 *garlic clove, minced*

1 *large ripe tomato*
2 *teaspoons chopped fresh basil*
2 *teaspoons chopped fresh parsley*
Salt and freshly ground black pepper

1. Scrub the zucchini and slice into ¼-inch rounds.
2. Heat the oil in a large skillet. Add the onion and garlic and cook for 10 minutes over very low heat, taking care not to brown the onion.
3. Core the tomato, halve crosswise, and scoop out some of the seeds with a melon baller or small spoon. Chop the tomato coarsely.
4. Add the zucchini to the skillet and cook over low heat, stirring frequently to prevent any vegetables from sticking. After 2 minutes, add the basil and parsley. When the zucchini is almost tender, add the chopped tomato and salt and pepper to taste.
5. Cover the skillet and continue cooking for 3 to 4 minutes. Serve immediately.

4 SERVINGS

Sautéed Zucchini with Herbs

Zucchini are always available, but they'll be at their best when they're being harvested where you live. Get tender 4-inch ones for this dish and enjoy the sweetness of simplicity.

½ cup unbleached all-purpose flour
2 teaspoons minced fresh rosemary
2 teaspoons minced fresh parsley
1 teaspoon minced fresh thyme
6 small zucchini, washed but not peeled
2 tablespoons extra virgin olive oil
1 tablespoon butter
1 garlic clove, minced
2 shallots, minced

1. In a shallow pan, combine the flour, rosemary, parsley, and thyme.
2. Slice the zucchini into ¼-inch rounds.
3. Heat the oil and butter in a large skillet and add the garlic and shallots. Cook over low heat for 2 minutes.
4. Dredge the zucchini slices in the flour mixture, shaking off any excess, and place in a single layer in the skillet. Turn up the heat slightly and brown on both sides, taking care not to let the zucchini stick (you may need to add oil or butter).

4 SERVINGS

Baked Squash with
Black Beans and Basil

You could serve this as a side dish on a buffet or for supper — or make more and have it as the centerpiece of the meal. Small (4-inch) summer squash and zucchini are young and tender, but larger, older ones will do.

3 small yellow squash, scrubbed and chopped
2 zucchini, scrubbed and chopped
1 cup cooked black beans, rinsed and drained
1 medium onion, chopped
1 garlic clove, minced
2 tablespoons dry white wine
1 tablespoon extra virgin olive oil
1 tablespoon balsamic vinegar
2 tablespoons chopped fresh basil
2 tablespoons chopped fresh parsley
Salt and freshly ground black pepper
2 tablespoons grated Parmesan cheese

1. Preheat the oven to 350°F and lightly oil the bottom of a 2½-quart baking dish.
2. In a large bowl, gently combine both kinds of squash, the black beans, onion, and garlic. Transfer the mixture to the baking dish.
3. In the same bowl, stir together the wine, oil, vinegar, basil, parsley, and salt and pepper to taste. Pour over the squash-and-beans mixture and sprinkle the cheese on top.
4. Bake for 30 to 35 minutes or until the squash is tender but not mushy.

4 SERVINGS

In many ancient cultures, basil was revered as having magical powers.

Zucchini with Linguine

Every now and then you need to force yourself to abandon red sauce for pasta and try something different. This linguine combines zucchini and oregano with the sharpness of lemon for a new view of spaghetti sauce.

2 tablespoons extra virgin olive oil
2 shallots, minced
2 garlic cloves, minced
½ sweet red pepper, finely chopped
1 cup chicken broth
¼ cup dry white wine
1 medium zucchini (enough for 2 cups), shredded
Zest of 1 lemon
Salt and freshly ground black pepper
1 pound fresh linguine or dried if fresh unavailable
3 tablespoons finely chopped fresh oregano
1 cup grated Parmesan cheese

1. Bring a large pot of water to a boil for the pasta.
2. Heat the oil in a medium-sized skillet. Add the shallots and garlic and cook, stirring, over low heat for about 2 minutes or until soft. Mix in the red pepper, broth, and wine and cook until the pepper is tender.

3. Add the zucchini to the skillet and cook for about 2 more minutes. Stir in the lemon zest and salt and pepper to taste. Remove from the heat.
4. Cook the linguine in the boiling water until al dente. Drain and transfer to a heated serving bowl.
5. Pour the sauce over the pasta, add the chopped oregano and cheese, and toss.

4 SERVINGS

Oregano has been used to calm upset stomachs since the time of the pharaohs.

Baked Butternut Squash and Oregano

A mellow winter squash can be happily married with various fruits. Here, ingredients of similar color visually blend together and create a casserole surprise, with extra zest provided by oregano.

½ tablespoon extra virgin olive oil
3 sweet turkey sausages (optional)
1 butternut squash, peeled and sliced
1 ripe mango, peeled and sliced
2 ripe peaches, peeled and sliced
Zest of 1 navel orange
Zest of 1 lemon
¼ cup minced fresh oregano
½ cup melted butter
½ cup sugar
¼ cup molasses

1. Heat the oil in a small skillet. Remove the casings from the turkey sausage and crumble the meat into the skillet. Brown, stirring frequently with a fork to separate the clumps.
2. Preheat the oven to 350°F. Spread the sausage in the bottom of a 2½-quart baking dish and arrange slices of squash, mango, and peaches over the sausage.

3. Mix the orange and lemon zests with the oregano and sprinkle over the fruit.
4. Combine the butter, sugar, and molasses and pour over the casserole. Cover and bake for 45 to 60 minutes or until the fruits and squash are fork tender.

4–5 SERVINGS

Grilled Zucchini with Tarragon

Ken Almgren, chef/owner of the elegant Federal House in South Lee, Massachusetts, uses very plump, 8-inch zucchini for this dish, and in season he harvests the tarragon from his own herb garden. At home he cooks the squash on the charcoal grill; at the restaurant he uses the indoor broiler.

> 2 *medium zucchini*
> 2 *teaspoons extra virgin olive oil*
> 1 *tablespoon lightly chopped fresh tarragon*
> ½ *teaspoon salt*
> *Pinch of black pepper (about four turns on a*
>   *pepper mill)*

1. Wash the zucchini and slice them at a slight angle into ½-inch pieces. Place in a large bowl.
2. While gently tossing the slices, drizzle the oil over them to coat.
3. Sprinkle on the tarragon, add the salt and pepper, and set aside to marinate for at least 30 minutes, up to 3 hours.
4. Place the zucchini slices on a charcoal grill at medium high heat. After 1 minute, rotate the slices 45° so that the grilling marks will form an X. After 1 more minute, turn the slices over and cook for another 2 minutes maximum. The zucchini should be al dente. Serve with the X side up. If using an oven broiler, cook the zucchini about 4 inches away from the heat for about the same amount of time.

4 SERVINGS

The flavor of perennial
Russian tarragon improves the longer
it grows in one spot.

Acorn Squash with Oranges and Mint

The very shape of an acorn squash makes it an appealing vegetable to stuff.
This version with oranges, mint, and rum offers a new twist.

2 acorn squash

2 oranges

½ lemon

8 tablespoons brown sugar

2 tablespoons minced fresh mint

4 tablespoons dark rum

2 tablespoons butter

4 tablespoons coarsely chopped walnuts

Salt and freshly ground black pepper

1. Preheat the oven to 375°F. Lightly grease a large, shallow baking dish.
2. Wash the acorn squash, halve lengthwise, and scoop out the seeds and any stringy pulp. Arrange the halves cut side up in the baking dish.
3. Wash the oranges and lemon, cut into thick slices, unpeeled, and remove all seeds and any extra pith.
4. Place 2 orange slices and 1 lemon slice in each squash half. If necessary, slit the edge of the orange slices to make them fit. In order, divide the sugar, mint, rum, butter, and walnuts in layers over the fruit. Sprinkle with salt and pepper to taste.

5. Cover the baking dish tightly with foil and bake for 30 to 45 minutes or until the squash is tender.

4 SERVINGS

Squash Casserole with Mint

It's hard to imagine anything but good coming from a recipe that includes graham crackers and brown sugar. Add squash, mint, and a little ginger, and the casserole becomes irresistible.

2 cups puréed acorn or butternut squash

2 tablespoons extra virgin olive oil

4 shallots, minced

½-inch fresh gingerroot, peeled and finely shredded

1 cup low-fat milk, room temperature

2 eggs, beaten

Salt and freshly ground black pepper

¾ cup crumbled graham crackers

2 tablespoons minced fresh mint

2 tablespoons minced fresh thyme

3 tablespoons dark brown sugar

¼ cup finely chopped pecans

2 tablespoons softened butter

1. Prepare the squash according to the directions on page 182, then purée.
2. Preheat the oven to 350°F and lightly grease a baking dish or soufflé.
3. In a small skillet, heat the oil and slowly cook the shallots and gingerroot until they are tender but not browned.
4. In a large bowl, combine the shallots and ginger with the milk, eggs, salt and pepper to taste, and the squash. Pour the mixture into the baking dish.
5. Combine the graham crackers, mint, thyme, brown sugar, and nuts. Sprinkle over the squash mixture. Dot with the butter. Bake for 30 to 35 minutes.

4 SERVINGS

Spicy Squash with Cilantro

Most recipes for zucchini and summer squash call for small ones — that means tender ones 4 to 6 inches long. Larger ones will have plenty of flavor but may need a little extra cooking or peeling.

6 small zucchini
1 tomato, ripe but firm
1 large white onion, finely chopped
1 tablespoon chopped fresh cilantro
2 tablespoons chopped fresh flat-leaf parsley
1 garlic clove, minced

¼ cup chopped green chili peppers
½ cup white wine
½ cup water
¼ cup pitted, chopped black olives
1 cup shredded Monterey Jack cheese
Salt and freshly ground black pepper

1. Bring a saucepan of water to a boil.
2. Scrub the zucchini and cut into ¼-inch slices. Drop the tomato into the boiling water for about 20 seconds, remove and rinse with cold water, and peel. Cut crosswise, remove some of the seeds, and dice.
3. In a large, deep skillet or saucepan, combine the zucchini, tomato, onion, cilantro, parsley, garlic, chili peppers, wine, and water. Mix well and cook over medium heat for 30 minutes or until the zucchini is tender.
4. Stir in the olives and cheese and add salt and pepper to taste. Continue stirring over low heat until the cheese is melted. Serve immediately.

4 SERVINGS

Acorn Squash with Dill and Sage

Centuries ago it was believed that sage promoted long life. When used with winter squash, sage may have little to do with longevity, but it *will* add flavor to the cold season. Try this combination in which the bite of dill lightens the taste of sage.

1 acorn squash
Olive oil
2 sweet potatoes
1 rib of celery, finely chopped
½ teaspoon salt
1 tablespoon minced fresh sage
2 tablespoons minced fresh dill
Freshly ground black pepper
½ cup orange juice
¼ cup brown sugar
¼ cup honey
1 tablespoon butter

1. Preheat the oven to 350°F and lightly grease a 1½-quart casserole.
2. Halve the squash lengthwise and remove the seeds and stringy fibers. Brush the cut edges with oil and place them cut side down on a baking sheet. Bake for 35 to 45 minutes. (Cooking time could be shortened using a microwave; follow instructions for your appliance.)

3. Peel and quarter the sweet potatoes. Place in a saucepan with the celery, cover with water, add the salt, and cook for 20 to 25 minutes or until tender. Drain and mash.

4. Turn the oven up to 375°F. Scoop out the squash flesh, mash, and add to the sweet potato and celery mixture. Stir in the sage, dill, pepper to taste, orange juice, sugar, and honey. Transfer the mixture to the greased baking dish.

5. Dot with butter and bake for 25 to 30 minutes.

6 SERVINGS

Zucchini Moussaka

For a hearty, mint-flavored lamb classic, try this casserole that has the warmth of chili powder, a hint of thyme, and the spice of cinnamon. Vine-ripened tomatoes will be an asset for this dish.

2 pounds lean ground lamb
1 large onion, chopped
3 garlic cloves, minced
4 large ripe tomatoes, coarsely chopped
½ cup tomato sauce
¼ teaspoon chili powder
2 teaspoons minced fresh lemon thyme
½ teaspoon ground cinnamon
2 tablespoons chopped fresh mint
Salt and freshly ground black pepper
½ pound shredded Monterey Jack cheese
¼ cup extra virgin olive oil
8 cups thickly sliced zucchini

1. Preheat the oven to 350°F and lightly oil a deep baking dish.
2. In a large skillet, cook the ground lamb, onion, and garlic for about 10 to 12 minutes or until the meat is browned and the onion is soft.
3. Drain off the fat and add the tomatoes, tomato sauce, chili powder, lemon thyme, cinnamon, mint, and salt and pepper to taste. Mix well and bring to a boil.
4. Reduce the heat and simmer for about 40 minutes. Remove the skillet from the heat, stir in half of the cheese, and set aside.
5. In another large skillet, heat the oil and sauté the zucchini slices until crisply tender. Place a layer of the zucchini in the baking dish, followed by a layer of the meat mixture, then a layer of cheese.
6. Repeat each layer, ending with zucchini. Sprinkle any remaining cheese on top and bake for 30 minutes.

6–8 SERVINGS

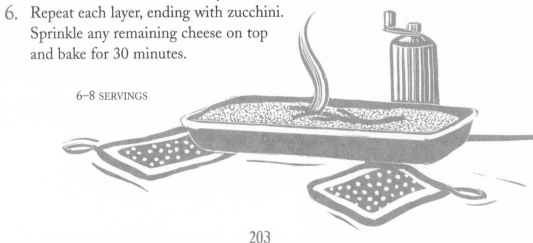

203

Spaghetti Squash with Basil and Parsley

Spaghetti squash is not an oxymoron. It is indeed a squash, and it both looks like and can be used like spaghetti. Cook this odd member of the squash family in the microwave oven, then toss it with herbs and fresh tomatoes.

> 1 medium spaghetti squash
> 2 large ripe tomatoes
> ¼ cup chopped fresh basil
> ¼ cup chopped fresh parsley
> 2 tablespoons extra virgin olive oil
> ½ teaspoon freshly ground black pepper
> ¼ teaspoon salt
> ¼ cup grated Parmesan cheese
> 2 tablespoons grated Romano cheese

1. Scrub the squash and pierce the skin in a number of places with a sharp knife, sharp fork, or knitting needle so that steam can escape during cooking. In the microwave, place the squash on a paper towel and cook it on high for 8 minutes. Turn it over and cook for another 10 minutes or until tender. Remove and set aside for about 10 minutes.
2. Meanwhile, bring a saucepan of water to a boil. Drop the tomatoes into the boiling water for about 20 seconds, remove, rinse with cold water, and peel. Halve them crosswise and remove some of the seeds with a melon baller. Chop coarsely.

3. In a small bowl, toss the basil, parsley, oil, pepper, and salt.
4. Halve the squash crosswise and scoop out the seeds. Unwind the spaghetti-like flesh with a fork and pile into a large bowl or colorful pasta dish.
5. Pour the tomatoes over the squash. Add the herb mixture and toss gently. Sprinkle some of the cheeses over the top and serve the rest on the side. Serve immediately.

4–6 SERVINGS

Squash Stir-Fry with Dill

Preparing vegetables and herbs the Asian way means careful planning, quick cooking, and crisp eating. With yellow and green squash, the flavor is delicate to begin with — and taking it easy on the cooking keeps the taste intact. To make this recipe work, have all ingredients measured and at hand before heating the wok.

> 3 *yellow summer squash, 4 to 6 inches long*
> 2 *zucchini, 4 inches long*
> 2 *tablespoons peanut oil*
> 1 *medium onion, cut into eighths*
> 2 *garlic cloves, chopped*
> ½ *teaspoon sesame oil*
> 2 *tablespoons light soy sauce*
> ½ *teaspoon sugar*
> ¼ *cup finely snipped fresh dill*
> 2 *tablespoons finely chopped fresh parsley*
> *Salt and freshly ground black pepper*

1. Scrub the summer squash and zucchini and remove the stem and blossom ends, but do not peel. Slice them into 2-inch sticks about ⅛ inch thick.
2. Heat a wok or large skillet until a drop of water skitters across the surface. Add the peanut oil, turning the pan so that all the surfaces are coated. Add the onion and garlic and cook, tossing continuously with a spatula, for 1 minute.
3. Add the squash and toss rapidly for 1 minute. Add the sesame oil, soy sauce, and sugar and continue to stir and cook for 1 more minute. Add the dill, parsley, and salt and pepper to taste, tossing until the herbs are mixed in and hot. Serve immediately.

5–6 SERVINGS

Herbed Squash with Chicken

Select the plumper zucchini or summer squash for this dish because they'll be used like dugout canoes. Garlic, parsley, and oregano give the chicken some zest. Turkey, of course, could be used as an alternative.

3 medium summer squash or zucchini
2 tablespoons extra virgin olive oil
3 scallions, white and green parts, chopped
1 garlic clove, minced
2 crimini mushrooms, finely chopped
2 tablespoons chopped fresh parsley
2 tablespoons chopped fresh oregano
¼ cup grated Swiss cheese
¼ cup plain bread crumbs
1 cup chopped cooked breast of chicken

1. Preheat the oven to 350°F and lightly grease a shallow baking dish. Bring a large pot of water to a boil.
2. Split the squash lengthwise, removing the stems carefully. Scoop out the seeds and then deepen the cavity with a sharp knife, taking care to leave a solid lining. Discard the seeds and reserve the flesh.
3. Drop the squash halves into the boiling water and cook for no more than 3 minutes. Drain and set aside.

4. In a skillet, heat the oil, add the scallions and garlic, and cook for 2 minutes, stirring constantly. Mix in the mushrooms and cook for 3 more minutes, stirring frequently. Chop the squash flesh and add it along with the parsley, oregano, cheese, and bread crumbs. Cook for another 2 minutes. Stir in the chicken until well combined and remove from the heat.

5. Stuff the squash canoes with the mixture, place in the baking dish, and bake for 30 minutes.

6 SERVINGS

Zucchini Frittata with Savory

Experiment with summer savory and winter savory. They're first cousins, so they're both alike and unalike. Incidentally, some herbalists consider summer savory an aphrodisiac. Whether that's true or not, this frittata will excite your taste buds at brunch, lunch, or supper.

2 medium zucchini, scrubbed and
   unpeeled
½ teaspoon salt
1 tablespoon extra virgin olive oil
2 tablespoons butter
3 scallions, white and green parts,
   minced
1 garlic clove, minced
8 eggs
¼ cup grated Parmesan cheese

1 tablespoon minced fresh savory
1 tablespoon minced fresh parsley
2 tablespoons butter
Salt and freshly ground black pepper

1. Slice the zucchini into ¼-inch rounds, place in a colander and sprinkle with the ½ teaspoon of salt, and let stand for at least 15 minutes.
2. In a large skillet, heat the oil and butter. Add the scallions and garlic and cook over low heat until tender but not browned.
3. Lightly squeeze the zucchini slices to remove moisture, add them to the skillet, spreading them evenly over the pan, and cook until they are slightly browned.
4. In the meantime, beat the eggs until foamy. Stir half of the cheese into the eggs, along with the savory and parsley.
5. Add the butter to the skillet with the vegetables and stir until the butter melts. Pour in the eggs and continue to cook over low heat, without stirring, until the eggs set. The top may still be runny.
6. Preheat the broiler. Sprinkle salt and pepper to taste and the remaining cheese over the eggs. Put the skillet under the broiler for 1 minute or until the frittata browns a little and puffs up.

4 SERVINGS

Patty Pan Squash with Rosemary and Thyme

The small white summer squash with their scalloped edges are so decorative that they almost ask to be stuffed and served whole — especially when the stuffing is colorful and nicely flavored with aromatic rosemary and thyme. Winter scalloped squash can be substituted but will need to be boiled twice as long and then baked for 45 minutes.

6 patty pan squash, 3 to 4 inches in diameter
2 tablespoons butter
2 medium onions, finely chopped
½ cup minced fresh parsley
3 cups grated carrots
2 garlic cloves, minced
½ cup white wine
1 teaspoon minced fresh thyme
½ teaspoon minced fresh rosemary
4 ounces cream cheese, cubed
Juice of ½ lime
Salt and freshly ground black pepper

1. Preheat the oven to 350°F. Bring a large pot of water to a boil.
2. Drop the squash whole into the boiling water for 10 to 12 minutes. Drain, cover with cold water, and drain again. Cut off the stem end of each squash, scoop out some of the flesh, and discard.
3. In a large skillet, melt the butter and cook the onions for 2 minutes. Add the parsley, carrots, garlic, and wine. Cook, stirring constantly, until the liquid is nearly gone. Add the thyme, rosemary, cream cheese, and lime juice.
4. Heat the mixture until the cheese melts and season with salt and pepper to taste. Spoon the filling into the squash, arrange on a baking sheet, and bake for 30 minutes or until hot.

6 SERVINGS

Summer Squash Tart with Sage

Things served in a crust have a certain mystique, especially when they're not dessert. Try this baking-powder-biscuit crust with succulent yellow squash as a main dish for lunch or supper. Fresh sage is essential for this recipe.

FOR THE CRUST
2 cups unbleached all-purpose flour
2 teaspoons baking powder
½ teaspoon salt
½ stick butter
⅔ cup milk

1. Sift together the flour, baking powder, and salt. Cut in the butter or blend the flour mixture and butter in a food processor.
2. Gradually add the milk. (Use a little more if needed to get a soft dough.) On a lightly floured board, knead the dough for 20 seconds. Roll it out to a ¼-inch thickness and place in a 10-inch pie pan, crimping the edges like pie pastry.

FOR THE FILLING

    3 yellow summer squash
    4 tablespoons butter, melted
    ½ cup unseasoned bread crumbs
    3 shallots, minced
    2 eggs, lightly beaten or ½ cup egg substitute
    2 tablespoons minced fresh sage
    Salt and freshly ground black pepper

1. Bring a pot of water to a boil. Preheat the oven to 375°F.
2. Scrub and chop the summer squash into 1-inch chunks. Boil, covered, for 8 minutes. Drain and mash well.
3. Combine the melted butter and bread crumbs in a large bowl. After stirring, remove 2 tablespoons of the mixture and reserve for a topping. Add the squash purée, shallots, eggs or egg substitute, sage, and salt and pepper to taste to the bowl and stir well.
4. Pour the mixture into the biscuit shell, sprinkle the reserved buttery crumbs on top, and bake for 45 minutes.

4–5 SERVINGS

Herbed Pork with Butternut Squash

A succulent pork tenderloin goes a long way because it has little extra fat and no bones. Try it in this casserole with a bouquet of herbs and a hint of Chinese cuisine.

1 *pork tenderloin*
1 *tablespoon soy sauce*
½ *tablespoon brown sugar*
  ½-inch fresh gingerroot, shredded
1 *teaspoon cornstarch*
1 *small butternut squash*
  Zest of 1 orange
1 *crisp apple, chopped*
1 *tablespoon chopped fresh marjoram*
2 *tablespoons chopped fresh parsley*
1 *tablespoon chopped fresh dill*
  Salt and white pepper
½ *cup dry white wine or Chinese rice wine*

1. Cut the pork into ¼-inch slices and place in a medium-sized bowl. In a cup or small bowl, combine the soy sauce, brown sugar, gingerroot, and cornstarch and pour over the pork. Toss to coat well, cover tightly with plastic wrap, and refrigerate for at least 1 hour, preferably 2.
2. When ready to prepare the dish, preheat the oven to 350°F. Peel the squash, remove the seeds and any stringy pulp, and cut into ½-inch chunks.
3. Place the pork and its marinade in a 2-quart baking dish, add the squash, orange zest, apple, marjoram, parsley, dill, and salt and white pepper to taste and stir to combine with the pork.
4. Pour in the wine, cover, and bake for 35–40 minutes. Uncover and bake for another 10 minutes or until the pork is tender.

4 SERVINGS

Yellow Squash with Curry

Curry is a mixture of spices. Combined here with mint and yogurt, the result is a cool hot dish or a hot cool dish, depending on how your taste buds react. Either way, it's delectable — especially when yellow summer squash are fresh from the garden.

2 tablespoons butter

1 medium onion, thinly sliced

2–2½ pounds yellow summer squash, scrubbed and unpeeled

3 tablespoons hot water

1¼ teaspoons curry powder

2 tablespoons finely chopped fresh mint

4 drops hot chili oil

Salt and freshly ground black pepper

¾ cup plain yogurt

1. In a large skillet, melt the butter over low heat and cook the onion for about 10 minutes or until translucent but not browned. Stir frequently.

2. Cut the squash into ¼-inch slices and add the squash and hot water to the onions. Heat to boiling, cover, reduce the heat to low, and simmer for another 10 minutes.

3. Stir in the curry powder, mint, chili oil, and salt and pepper to taste and cook uncovered for another 10 minutes, stirring frequently. Add the yogurt and reheat, but do not boil. Serve immediately.

4 SERVINGS

Minted Squash Cookies

Fruits and vegetables add extra moistness to breads, cakes, and cookies. These delectable drop cookies, which can be quickly mixed in a food processor, keep well or travel well.

¾ cup butter
1 cup sugar
1 egg
1½ cups unbleached all-purpose flour
½ teaspoon baking soda
½ teaspoon salt
1 teaspoon cinnamon
¼ teaspoon ground ginger

1¾ cups rolled oats
1½ cups puréed winter squash
2 squares semisweet chocolate, shaved
2 tablespoons minced fresh mint

1. Heat the oven to 400°F.
2. In a food processor, combine the butter, sugar, egg, flour, baking soda, salt, cinnamon, ginger, rolled oats, and squash. Process until well mixed.
3. Mix the chocolate shavings and minced mint and fold into the cookie mixture. Drop rounded teaspoons of batter onto a cookie sheet and bake for 12 to 15 minutes or until browned.

ABOUT 4 DOZEN COOKIES

Zucchini Cake with Rose Petals

With zucchini for moisture and rose flavors for delicacy, this cake takes on a garden air that's quite special. You may want to make your own rose petal vinegar, but a high-quality white wine vinegar can be used as a substitute.

FOR THE CAKE

- 1 cup butter, softened
- 2 cups sugar
- 4 large eggs
- 1½ cups zucchini, shredded
- 2 tablespoons minced fresh, unsprayed rose geranium leaves
- 2 tablespoons minced fresh, unsprayed rose petals

- 3 cups unbleached all-purpose flour
- 1½ teaspoons baking soda
- 1½ teaspoons ground cardamom
- ½ teaspoon salt
- ¼ cup buttermilk
- ⅓ cup rose-petal or white-wine vinegar
- 1 cup slivered almonds, finely chopped and dusted with flour

1. Preheat the oven to 350°F. Grease and flour a 10-inch tube or Bundt pan.
2. In a large bowl, cream the butter and sugar until fluffy. Add the eggs one at a time, beating well after each one. Mix in zucchini, rose geranium leaves, and rose petals. A food processor can be used.
3. Sift the flour, baking soda, cardamom, and salt into a separate bowl. Add some of the flour mixture and then some of the buttermilk and vinegar to the egg mixture, beating after each addition. Continue until all are combined. Stir in the almonds.

4. Pour into the prepared cake pan and bake for 1 hour or until a toothpick inserted in the cake comes out clean. Cool for 10 minutes in the pan and invert onto a rack.

FOR THE FROSTING

1 tablespoon butter
2 tablespoons milk
4 drops red food coloring

1 cup confectioners' sugar
1 teaspoon vanilla

1. Melt the butter in a medium-size saucepan.
2. Stir in the milk and food coloring and sift the sugar into the mixture. Add the vanilla and stir well. If the mixture is too stiff, add more milk. Drizzle over the cooled cake.

ROSE-PETAL VINEGAR

To be sure you are using pesticide-free flowers, use only unsprayed, untreated rose petals from your own garden.

1 cup loosely packed rose petals
2 cups white-wine vinegar

1. Place the petals in a glass or ceramic bowl, cover them with the vinegar, seal the container tightly, and store in a dark place at room temperature.
2. After a week, check the flavor. The brew can be steeped for several weeks if you want a stronger taste. When the flavor is right for you, strain the mixture, pour into a bottle, add a couple of fresh petals, and seal until needed.

Squash Pie with Rosemary

A friend who was a counterman at an old-fashioned diner was always a salesman, so when a customer asked for a piece of squash pie, he would serve it right up. If the next person on the stool wanted pumpkin pie, it came from the same pie plate. My mother, however, says pumpkin pie is never as good as squash and that she can tell the difference.

1 butternut squash (2 cups of purée)
Safflower or canola oil
Pastry for a 1-crust, 9-inch pie
3 eggs
½ cup brown sugar, packed
½ cup granulated sugar
¾ teaspoon ground ginger
¼ teaspoon ground nutmeg
½ teaspoon ground cinnamon
1 teaspoon vanilla extract

1 tablespoon molasses
2 teaspoons minced fresh rosemary
1 cup half-and-half

1. Preheat the oven to 375°F. Scrub the squash and halve it lengthwise, removing the seeds and any stringy pulp. Lightly brush the cut surfaces with oil and place them cut side down on a baking sheet. Bake for 40 to 60 minutes, testing occasionally to see if the squash is tender.

2. Remove the squash from the oven and let cool for a few minutes. Scoop out the flesh and either mash it smooth or purée it in a blender or food processor. Measure 2 cups and reserve the rest for bread or biscuits.

3. Prepare the pastry shell with a high, fluted rim, and refrigerate while making the filling.

4. Reheat the oven to 425°F.

5. In a large bowl, beat the eggs lightly. Add the sugars, ginger, nutmeg, cinnamon, vanilla, molasses, and rosemary, beating well. Add the squash and the half-and-half and beat again until the filling is well blended.

6. Pour into the chilled pie shell and bake in the lower half of the oven for 10 minutes. Reduce the heat to 350°F and cook for another 45 minutes. When a table knife inserted near the center comes out clean, the pie is done.

7. Serve plain, with whipped cream, or with a dollop of sour cream.

6–8 SERVINGS

Index

Converting Recipe Measurements to Metric

Use the following formulas for converting U.S. measurements to metric. Since the conversions are not exact, it's important to convert the measurements for all of the ingredients to maintain the same proportions as the original recipe.

WHEN THE MEASUREMENT GIVEN IS	MULTIPLY IT BY	TO CONVERT TO
teaspoons	4.93	milliliters
tablespoons	14.79	milliliters
fluid ounces	29.57	milliliters
cups (liquid)	236.59	milliliters
cups (liquid)	.236	liters
cups (dry)	275.31	milliliters
cups (dry)	.275	liters
pints (liquid)	473.18	milliliters
pints (liquid)	.473	liters
pints (dry)	550.61	milliliters
pints (dry)	.551	liters
quarts (liquid)	946.36	milliliters
quarts (liquid)	.946	liters
quarts (dry)	1101.22	milliliters
quarts (dry)	1.101	liters
gallons	3.785	liters
ounces	28.35	grams
pounds	.454	kilograms
inches	2.54	centimeters
degrees Fahrenheit (Centigrade)	$\frac{5}{9}$ (temperature − 32)	degrees Celsius

While standard metric measurements for dry ingredients are given as units of mass, U.S. measurements are given as units of volume. Therefore, the conversions listed above for dry ingredients are given in the metric equivalent of volume.